Sanjeev Kapoor

Wedding COLLECTION

Recipes for Newly-weds

Popular Prakashan
www.popularprakashan.com

Published by:

POPULAR PRAKASHAN PVT. LTD.
301, Mahalaxmi Chambers
22, Bhulabhai Desai Road
Mumbai 400 026
for KHANA KHAZANA PUBLICATIONS PVT. LTD.

First Published 2010

(4351)
ISBN – 978-81-7991-603-2

Book Design: Pratibha Gurnani Creative

Photography: Bharat Bhirangi, Alim Bolar

Food Stylist: Anupa Das

Printed in India
by Thomson Press (I) Ltd.
New Delhi

author's note

Marriages, they say, are made in heaven. But being a happily married man for the past 18 years to gorgeous Alyona, I would add, 'Marriages are enriched and strengthened at the dining table!' Food has a wonderful way of uniting people – a meal prepared and enjoyed together creates bonds and memories that will last forever. Every dish, every meal has a story or evokes a memory. The history of a romance and a marriage can very often be recorded and described by the meals one has enjoyed as a couple.

This book is one that I hope will make memories for you in your new life together. There are ideas in here for intimate meals: frothy Mushroom Cappuccino will have you licking your lips, exotic Black Grape Pani Puri will make you drool for more, and Stir-fried Chicken with Chillies and Basil will add a touch of heat and spice to the occasion.

Entertaining friends and relatives in your new home can be nerve-wracking. I have made it easier for you by giving you recipes to wow your in-laws and win over your partner's friends with a selection of delicious fare that is designed to impress. Turn out a tropical Virgin Piña Colada accompanied by exotic Chao Tom (Prawns on Sugarcane Sticks); Garlic-Chilli Crabs and Spicy Chicken Fried Rice on Basil Leaves; and for a grand finale, present a show-stopping Tiramisù or Chocolate Nut Fondue!

There are recipes for those times you just want to chill out with your pals over something quick and casual, and something cool to wash it all down with. Crisp Mexican Chaat, tongue-searing Chicken 65 and a chilled Kokum and Anar Slush will help you to do just that.

If it's comfort food you are looking for when you just want to pamper yourselves with something soul-satisfying, cook up some speedy Sindhi Kadhi to smother a heaping portion of rice, or a steaming bowl of aromatic Chicken Laksa. But if you want to cut back on the calories without sacrificing the taste, choose the no-oil Mutton Dhansaak or Penne Arrabbiata.

When the mehndi has faded, the strains of the shehnai are becoming a beautiful memory, and the frenetic excitement of the wedding has settled into a gentle routine, reach for this book to create delicious memories that will last a lifetime.

Wishing you many years of married bliss, and remember, a couple that eats together, stays together!

Sanjeev Kapoor

contents

beverages

melon and mango smoothie

1 medium-sized ripe musk melon

2 ripe Alphonso mangoes

2 tablespoons strawberry crush

1 cup crushed ice

1 Cut the melon into wedges, peel and remove seeds. Chop half a wedge into half-inch cubes. Chop the remaining melon into one-inch cubes. Place in a freezer for an hour.

2 Peel the mangoes and chop one slice into half-inch cubes. Chop the remaining mango into one-inch cubes. Place in a freezer for an hour.

3 Place the large cubes of melon and mango in a blender with the strawberry crush and one cup of crushed ice. Blend till smooth and frothy.

4 Pour into individual glasses and serve, topped with the smaller melon and mango cubes.

virgin piña colada

1¾ cups (350 ml) unsweetened pineapple juice

8 tablespoons thick Coconut Milk (page 126)

8 tablespoons shredded tender coconut flesh

2 cups vanilla ice cream

8 tablespoons chopped pineapple chunks

16-20 tinned cherries

Crushed ice

1 Blend the pineapple juice, coconut milk, shredded coconut, vanilla ice cream and ice till smooth.

2 Pour into individual Collins glasses.

3 Serve immediately, decorated with pineapple chunks and cherries.

ginger lemonade

2 inches ginger, grated

3 tablespoons lemon juice

1 cup sugar

4 lemon slices

A few sprigs of mint

Ice cubes

1 Combine the ginger and sugar with two cups of water in a pan. Bring the mixture to a boil, stirring continuously till the sugar dissolves. Simmer for three minutes.

2 Strain the syrup through a piece of muslin and set aside to cool.

3 Combine the syrup with two and a half cups of water. Add the lemon juice and stir well.

4 Pour into tall glasses. Add ice cubes and mint leaves and decorate each glass with a lemon slice. Serve immediately.

green lady

8 tablespoons *khus* syrup

A pinch of salt

2 tablespoons lemon juice

4 glasses lemonade

4 lemon slices

Crushed ice

1 Mix together the *khus* syrup, salt and lemon juice.

2 Add the crushed ice and lemonade and stir well.

3 Garnish with a slice of lemon and serve chilled.

pink blush

1 cup cranberry juice, chilled

1 cup orange juice, chilled

2 teaspoons sugar syrup

2 cups club soda, chilled

4 canned cherries, to garnish

1 Combine the cranberry juice, orange juice, sugar syrup and club soda well.

2 Pour into individual glasses and serve chilled, decorated with a cherry.

virgin bloody mary

5 cups tomato juice

Salt as required

1 lemon, sliced

1 teaspoon celery salt

1 teaspoon white pepper powder

4 garlic cloves, chopped

1 teaspoon Tabasco sauce

10-12 ice cubes, crushed

Celery stalks, to garnish

1 Fill a saucer with salt. Wet the rims of individual Old-fashioned glasses with lemon slices and dip in the salt. Set aside.

2 Blend the tomato juice, celery salt, white pepper powder, garlic and Tabasco sauce till smooth. Add the crushed ice and blend again.

3 Strain into the salt-rimmed glasses and serve chilled, with celery stalks as swizzle sticks.

Kokum and Anar Slush

kokum and anar slush

1⅓ cup *kokum* syrup

2 teaspoons roasted cumin powder

2 teaspoons black salt

8 tablespoons sugar

4 cups crushed ice

4 tablespoons pomegranate kernels

1 Blend the *kokum* syrup, roasted cumin powder, black salt, sugar and crushed ice in a blender until slushy.

2 Pour into individual glasses and serve, decorated with a sprinkling of pomegranate kernels.

irish coffee

½ cup Irish whisky

3 teaspoons instant coffee powder

4 teaspoons sugar

¼ cup heavy cream, chilled

1 Add two teaspoons of sugar to the chilled cream and whip till it forms peaks. Set aside.

2 Pour three cups of water into a deep microwave-safe bowl and cover. Cook in a microwave oven on HIGH (100%) for five minutes or until steaming.

3 Remove from the oven, add the coffee powder and remaining two teaspoons of sugar and stir to dissolve. Stir in the whisky.

4 Pour the coffee into four stemmed glasses and top it with the whipped cream.

Chef's Tip: Replace the Irish whisky with mint liqueur for a different flavour.

coffee ambrosia

3 cups milk

4 teaspoons instant coffee powder

4 tablespoons sugar

4 small scoops vanilla ice cream

4 tablespoons Advocaat (liqueur)

1 Heat the milk and set aside.

2 To make the coffee, combine the coffee powder and sugar in a large bowl. Add two to three tablespoons of water and whisk for six to eight minutes till the mixture changes colour and turns creamy.

3 Pour the mixture into four large cups. Strain the milk and pour into the cups till three-fourth full and stir gently.

4 Gently place a scoop of ice cream on the coffee in each cup. Drizzle a tablespoon of Advocaat over the ice cream and serve immediately.

Coffee Ambrosia

strawberry and orange soya shake

4 tablespoons strawberry crush

1 orange

6 tablespoons orange squash

4 cups chilled soya milk

4 teaspoons sugar

4 scoops vanilla ice cream

2 cups crushed ice

1 Peel and remove the pith from the orange segments. Peel off the white membrane and separate the flakes. Place in the refrigerator to chill for ten minutes.

2 Place the strawberry crush, orange squash, soya milk, sugar and vanilla ice cream in a blender and process till smooth.

3 Place the crushed ice in four glasses. Pour the strawberry-soya shake over the ice.

4 Top with the orange flakes and serve immediately.

soups

chiang mai noodle soup

200 grams boneless chicken, cut into thin strips
200 grams egg noodles, blanched
1 tablespoon oil
1 tablespoon Red Curry Paste (page 127)
¼ teaspoon turmeric powder
4 cups Chicken Stock (page 126)
1 tablespoon fish sauce
18-20 black peppercorns, ground
Salt to taste
½ cup Coconut Milk (page 126)
1 tablespoon lemon juice

1 Heat the oil in a wok; add the chicken strips and sauté for five minutes.

2 Add the red curry paste and turmeric powder and sauté for another two minutes.

3 Add the chicken stock, fish sauce, ground peppercorns and salt and simmer for ten minutes, or until the chicken is cooked.

4 Stir in the coconut milk. Add the blanched noodles and remove from heat. Stir in the lemon juice and serve hot.

Chef's Tip: To blanch noodles, cook in boiling salted water till *al dente* (cooked, but still firm to the bite). Drain, refresh in cold water and drain again.

mushroom cappuccino

15 large fresh button mushrooms, thickly sliced

1 tablespoon butter

1 bay leaf

1 small onion, chopped

4-6 garlic cloves, chopped

4 cups Vegetable Stock (page 126)

Salt to taste

¼ teaspoon white pepper powder

¾ cup cream

2 cups milk, chilled

1 teaspoon cinnamon powder

1 Melt the butter in a heavy-bottomed pan. Add the bay leaf, onion and garlic and sauté for two to three minutes till the onion is translucent.

2 Add the mushrooms and sauté for one minute. Add one cup of vegetable stock and cook for five more minutes. Remove from heat and cool. Remove the bay leaf and discard.

3 Make a purée of the cooked mushrooms and add the remaining vegetable stock. Return to heat and bring to a boil. Add salt and white pepper powder, lower the heat and simmer for two to three minutes.

4 Stir in the cream and remove from heat. Pour the soup into individual cups and keep warm.

5 Pour the chilled milk into a chilled bowl. Beat with a fork till the milk develops a thick froth. Collect the froth with a ladle and place on the hot mushroom soup giving it a cappuccino effect.

6 Sprinkle cinnamon powder and serve immediately.

Chef's Tip: Use milk with a high fat content for a thick froth.

seafood soup

16 small (150 grams) prawns, peeled and deveined

1 small (200 grams) black pomfret, skinned, filleted and cut into ½-inch cubes

1 small squid, cut into rings

Salt to taste

5 cups Vegetable Stock (page 126)

1 lemon grass stalk, sliced diagonally

1 inch celery stalk, chopped

1 inch ginger, grated

¼ teaspoon black pepper powder

4 medium fresh button mushrooms, thinly sliced

2 fresh red chillies, thinly sliced

2 spring onion greens, sliced

½ teaspoon lemon juice

1 Blanch the prawns, fish and squid in three to four cups of boiling salted water for one minute. Drain, refresh in cold water and set aside.

2 Bring the vegetable stock to a boil in a wok. Lower heat, add the lemon grass, celery, ginger, salt, pepper and mushrooms, and simmer for two to three minutes.

3 Add the blanched seafood and fresh red chillies, cover and simmer for another two minutes.

4 Stir in the spring onion greens and lemon juice. Adjust seasoning, stir and simmer for one more minute.

5 Pour into soup bowls and serve hot.

prawn ball soup

250 grams prawns, shelled, deveined and minced

3-4 tinned bamboo shoot slices

Salt to taste

Black pepper powder to taste

1 tablespoon cornflour

1 egg white, beaten

1 tablespoon olive oil

1 inch ginger, chopped

5-6 medium fresh button mushrooms, sliced

5-6 black peppercorns, crushed

4 cups Chicken Stock (page 126)

10-12 fresh spinach leaves

2-3 stalks spring onion greens, chopped

1 Boil the bamboo shoots in two cups of water for three to four minutes. Drain and cut into strips. Set aside.

2 Add the salt and pepper powder to the prawns and mix. Add the cornflour and egg white. Mix well. Take a teaspoonful of the mixture and shape into a small ball. Repeat with the remaining mixture.

3 Heat the oil in a wok and sauté the ginger for half a minute. Add the bamboo shoot slices, mushrooms, crushed peppercorns, salt and chicken stock and bring to a boil.

4 Add the prawn balls and cook for two to three minutes. Add the spinach leaves and simmer for a minute.

5 Serve hot, garnished with spring onion greens.

Prawn Ball Soup

chicken coconut rasam

500 grams chicken bones

100 grams boneless chicken, cut into 1-inch cubes

½ cup grated coconut

3 tablespoons Tamarind Pulp (page 126)

2 medium tomatoes, roughly chopped

Salt to taste

2 tablespoons *rasam* powder

8 black peppercorns, crushed

1 teaspoon red chilli powder

½ teaspoon turmeric powder

15 curry leaves

2 tablespoons chopped fresh coriander

2 tablespoons olive oil

1 teaspoon mustard seeds

2-3 dried red chillies, broken into two

1 Grind the coconut with one cup of warm water. Extract the coconut milk and set aside. Reserve the coconut residue.

2 Boil the chicken bones in about six to seven cups of water for fifteen minutes.

3 Skim off the scum from the surface, add the tamarind pulp, tomatoes, chicken cubes, salt, *rasam* powder, crushed black peppercorns, chilli powder, turmeric powder and ten curry leaves. Simmer till the liquid reduces by half and a nice aroma is given out.

4 Add the drained coconut residue to the *rasam*. Sprinkle the chopped coriander and simmer for about three to four minutes.

5 Remove from heat and strain the *rasam*. Separate the chicken pieces from the residue and cut into half-inch cubes and reserve for garnish.

6 Reheat the strained *rasam*, add the coconut milk and simmer for a couple of minutes. Remove from heat and add chicken pieces to it.

7 Heat olive oil and add the mustard seeds, red chillies and remaining curry leaves. Add to the prepared soup and cover immediately to trap the flavours.

8 Serve piping hot. You can squeeze a lemon into the *rasam* to make it really tangy.

balinese vegetable soup

225 grams French beans, cut into ½-inch pieces
Salt to taste
2 cups thick Coconut Milk (page 126)
1 garlic clove
2 fresh red chillies, chopped
4 almonds
½ tablespoon coriander powder
2 tablespoons oil
1 medium onion, sliced
2 bay leaves
1⅓ cups bean sprouts
2 tablespoons lemon juice

1 Cook the French beans in six cups of boiling salted water for three to four minutes. Drain and reserve the cooking liquid.

2 Skim off four tablespoons of coconut cream from the top of the coconut milk and reserve.

3 Grind the garlic, fresh red chillies, almonds and coriander powder to a paste.

4 Heat the oil in a wok; add the onion and sauté till translucent. Drain and set aside.

5 To the same oil, add the ground paste and sauté without browning for about two minutes. Add the reserved cooking liquid and coconut milk. Bring to a boil and add the bay leaves. Cook, uncovered, for fifteen to twenty minutes.

6 Just before serving, stir in the beans, sautéed onion, bean sprouts, reserved coconut cream and lemon juice. Adjust the salt and serve immediately.

badam shorba

175 grams almonds

2 teaspoons butter

1¼ teaspoons refined flour

1 cup milk

½ teaspoon sugar

Salt to taste

¼ teaspoon white pepper powder

1½ tablespoons cream

1 Soak the almonds in hot water for a few minutes. Drain and peel. Slice ten or twelve almonds for garnishing and grind the rest to a smooth paste.

2 Melt the butter in a pan; add the flour and sauté for one minute. Gradually pour in the milk, stirring continuously to prevent lumps from forming.

3 Add the sugar, salt and white pepper powder and cook, stirring continuously, till the mixture comes to a boil. Lower the heat and simmer for five minutes, stirring occasionally.

4 Add the almond paste and two cups of hot water and simmer for ten to fifteen minutes, stirring occasionally, till the soup thickens.

5 Toast the sliced almonds. Sprinkle the toasted almonds and drizzle the cream over the soup just before serving piping hot.

salads

marinated prawn salad

15 medium prawns, cleaned and blanched

¼ cup grated coconut

4 shallots, sliced

2 lemon grass stalks, chopped

3 Kaffir lime leaves, finely shredded

A few fresh mint leaves, to garnish

Dressing

A pinch of brown sugar

4 tablespoons lemon juice

1 tablespoon fish sauce

2 fresh red chillies, chopped

1 garlic clove, chopped

Salt to taste

1 In a large bowl, toss together the prawns, coconut, shallots, lemon grass and lime leaves.

2 For the dressing, mix together the brown sugar, lemon juice, fish sauce, red chillies, garlic and salt in a small bowl.

3 Pour the dressing over the prawn and coconut mixture and toss gently to mix.

4 Serve, garnished with fresh mint leaves.

vegetable ribbons

1 medium zucchini, trimmed

2 medium carrots, trimmed

2 medium cucumbers, trimmed

1 inch celery stalk, chopped

Salt to taste

Dressing

2 tablespoons vinegar

1 tablespoon soy sauce

1 teaspoon brown sugar

¼ teaspoon red chilli flakes

3-4 fresh basil leaves, torn

Salt to taste

Garnish

5 medium black olives, sliced

1 With a potato peeler or a slicer, cut the zucchini, carrots and cucumbers lengthways into thin ribbons. Sprinkle a little salt and set aside for five minutes.

2 Process the vinegar, soy sauce, brown sugar, chilli flakes, basil leaves and salt in a blender to make a coarse paste. Transfer to a bowl.

3 Squeeze the juice released from the salted vegetables.

4 Add the vegetables to the dressing in the bowl along with the celery and toss well.

5 Serve garnished with olive slices.

Chef's Tip: Serve immediately as the zucchini tends to release water and lose its crispness.

Vegetable Ribbons

piquant potato salad

750 grams baby potatoes

Salt to taste

Dressing

3 tablespoons olive oil

1½ tablespoons white vinegar

7-8 peppercorns, crushed

1 teaspoon English mustard paste

2 pickled gherkins, finely chopped

1 tablespoon chopped fresh parsley

1 Scrub the potatoes clean, wash and place in a large pan with boiling salted water. Boil for fifteen to twenty minutes, or till just tender. Drain.

2 For the dressing, pour the olive oil and white vinegar into a small bowl; stir in salt to taste, crushed peppercorns, mustard paste, gherkins and parsley.

3 Place the potatoes in a large bowl and pour the dressing over while the potatoes are still warm. Stir gently to coat thoroughly with the dressing.

4 Leave to cool, but do not chill.

5 Serve in a shallow dish at room temperature.

carrot, raisin and black olive salad

4-5 large carrots

½ cup raisins

6-8 black olives, sliced

2 tablespoons lemon juice

5-6 black peppercorns, crushed

1 green chilli, finely chopped

1 tablespoon honey

Salt to taste

¼ teaspoon black salt

6 walnut kernels, crushed

1 teaspoon extra virgin olive oil

6- 8 fresh mint leaves

1 Thickly grate the carrots. Refrigerate till required for use.

2 Combine the lemon juice, crushed peppercorns, green chilli, honey, salt, black salt, walnuts, raisins, black olives and extra virgin olive oil to make a dressing.

3 Just before serving add the dressing to the grated carrots and toss. Serve garnished with mint leaves.

penne in thousand island dressing

1 cup penne (nib-shaped pasta), boiled

½ cup Thousand Island Dressing (see below)

1 medium carrot, cut into large pieces

¼ small broccoli, separated into small florets

3-4 French beans, cut diagonally into large pieces

1 tablespoon olive oil

½ medium green capsicum, cut into small triangles

1 medium onion, quartered

10-12 cherry tomatoes, halved

4-5 stuffed olives

1 Blanch the carrot, broccoli and French beans separately. Refresh in cold water and drain.

2 Toss the pasta in the olive oil in a large mixing bowl.

3 Add the capsicum, onion, blanched vegetables, cherry tomatoes and stuffed olives.

4 Pour in the Thousand Island dressing, toss lightly and serve chilled.

Thousand Island Dressing

¾ cup Mayonnaise (page 126)

1 tablespoon tomato ketchup

1 teaspoon Tabasco sauce

3-4 olives, stoned and finely chopped

2-3 pickled onions, finely chopped

2 pickled gherkins, finely chopped

1 Mix together the mayonnaise, tomato ketchup and Tabasco sauce in a bowl.

2 Add the olives, pickled onions and gherkins and mix well.

som tam

2 cups shredded unripe papaya

4 garlic cloves

Salt to taste

1 fresh red chilli, roughly chopped

4 cherry tomatoes, quartered

2 tablespoons lemon juice

2 tablespoons brown sugar

1 tablespoon soy sauce

½ tablespoon Tamarind Pulp (page 126)

½ cup roasted peanuts, crushed

1 Place the shredded papaya in a large bowl and crush lightly with a pestle.

2 Crush the garlic cloves and salt with a mortar and pestle. Add the red chilli and cherry tomatoes and continue to crush lightly.

3 Add the crushed garlic to the papaya with the lemon juice and mix well.

4 Crush the brown sugar with the mortar and pestle; add the soy sauce and tamarind pulp and mix well.

5 Add the mixture to the papaya and mix. Add the crushed roasted peanuts and toss to mix. Serve immediately.

Chef's Tip: You can use jaggery instead of the brown sugar.

mango sasam

3 medium ripe mangoes

¼ cup green grapes

¾ cup grated coconut

2 Bedgi chillies, seeded and roasted

¼ teaspoon mustard seeds

1 teaspoon Tamarind Pulp (page 126)

2 tablespoons grated jaggery

Salt to taste

1 Peel the mangoes, remove the seed and cut into one-inch cubes.

2 Grind together the coconut, red chillies, mustard seeds, tamarind pulp with one-fourth cup of water into a coarse paste. Add the jaggery and blend once again.

3 Place the mango cubes and grapes in a bowl. Add the salt and the ground *masala*.

4 Mix well and serve cold.

Note: When mangoes are not in season you can make the *sasam* with other fruit like ripe banana, orange, pineapple, apple etc.

fish and dill salad

250 grams fish fillets

A few sprigs of fresh dill, roughly chopped

4-5 peppercorns

1 bay leaf

2-inch celery stalk, roughly chopped

1 tablespoon lemon juice

Salt to taste

¼ teaspoon black peppercorns, crushed

2 tablespoons olive oil

1 medium capsicum, cut into half-inch diamonds

1 Cut the fish fillets into one-inch pieces.

2 Bring a little water to a boil in a shallow pan; add the peppercorns, bay leaf and celery. Add the fish and cook, uncovered, for two minutes or till the fish is just done. Remove from the water carefully and set aside to cool.

3 For the dressing, combine the lemon juice, salt, crushed peppercorns and olive oil in a bowl. Add the dill, reserving some for garnishing.

4 Arrange the poached fish cubes carefully in a bowl. Add the capsicum and pour the dressing over. Mix gently and serve chilled, garnished with reserved dill.

mango salad

1 large green unripe mango

1 large head of lettuce

1 cup chopped fresh coriander

1 fresh red chilli, seeded and chopped

2 shallots, chopped

2 tablespoons lemon juice

1 tablespoon light soy sauce

Salt to taste

1 Peel the mango and cut into long strips. Soak in iced water for ten minutes. Drain.

2 Line a large salad bowl with the lettuce leaves.

3 Combine the red chilli, shallots, lemon juice and soy sauce in a small bowl.

4 Mix the mango with the dressing and add the coriander leaves. Add salt to taste.

5 Transfer the salad to the bowl. Serve immediately.

tandoori murgh chaat

2 (150 grams each) boneless chicken breasts, skin removed

1 teaspoon Kashmiri chilli powder

1 teaspoon ginger paste

1 teaspoon garlic paste

½ cup drained yogurt

Salt to taste

1 tablespoon lemon juice

½ teaspoon *garam masala* powder

2 teaspoons mustard oil

2 tablespoons butter

1 small green capsicum, cut into thin strips

½ each small red and yellow capsicums, cut into thin strips

1 medium onion, sliced

2 green chillies, chopped

2 tablespoons fresh coriander, chopped

1 tablespoon lemon juice

1 teaspoon *chaat masala*

½ small unripe green mango (optional), chopped

1 Make incisions with a sharp knife on the chicken breasts and set aside.

2 Combine the chilli powder, ginger paste, garlic paste, drained yogurt, salt, lemon juice, *garam masala* powder and mustard oil. Spread the mixture over the chicken breasts and leave to marinate for three to four hours, preferably in a refrigerator.

3 Preheat the oven to 200°C/400°F/Gas mark 6. Thread the chicken onto skewers and cook for ten to twelve minutes, or until almost tender. Baste the chicken with butter and cook for another four minutes.

4 Remove from heat and shred the chicken when cool.

5 In a large bowl, combine the shredded chicken, all the capsicums, the onion, green chillies, half the chopped coriander, lemon juice, *chaat masala*, unripe mango and salt. Toss well to mix.

6 Transfer to a serving plate and serve, garnished with the remaining chopped coriander.

murgh aur shimla mirch salad

2 boneless chicken breasts

1 medium red capsicum, cut into strips

1 medium green capsicum, cut into strips

1 medium yellow capsicum, cut into strips

5-6 green olives

5-6 black olives

Marinade

1 tablespoon olive oil

3 tablespoons yogurt

½ tablespoon green chilli paste

1 teaspoon ginger-garlic paste

½ teaspoon *garam masala* powder

5-6 black peppercorns, crushed

Salt to taste

Dressing

4 teaspoons extra virgin olive oil

2 teaspoons lemon juice

2 teaspoons *chaat masala*

Black salt to taste

1 Mix all the ingredients for the marinade in a bowl. Add the chicken breasts and marinate, preferably in the refrigerator, for an hour.

2 Mix all the ingredients for the dressing and set aside.

3 Grill the chicken breasts in a pre-heated grill, or on a *tawa* on medium heat, for eight to ten minutes or until tender, turning once or twice, taking care they remain juicy. Cool and cut into one-inch pieces.

4 Add all the capsicums, the olives and the dressing. Toss lightly and serve immediately.

paneer and pineapple salad

300 grams cottage cheese, cut into ½-inch cubes

½ small fresh pineapple, cut into cubes

1 large unpeeled cucumber, cut into 1-inch pieces

1 medium green capsicum, cut into 1-inch pieces

½ small head of iceberg lettuce

6-8 black olives, stoned and sliced

1 teaspoon garlic paste

1 tablespoon lemon juice

1 teaspoon red chilli powder

½ teaspoon mixed dried herbs

Salt to taste

1½ tablespoons oil

Dressing

3 tablespoons salad oil

4 tablespoons vinegar

1 teaspoon sugar

1 teaspoon mustard powder

5-6 black peppercorns, crushed

½ teaspoon white pepper powder

1 Combine the garlic paste, lemon juice, chilli powder, dried herbs and salt. Rub the mixture into the cottage cheese pieces and set aside to marinate, preferably in a refrigerator, for fifteen to twenty minutes.

2 Mix together all the ingredients for the dressing in a bowl.

3 Thread the cottage cheese cubes onto skewers. Heat the oil on a *tawa* and place the skewers on it. Cook, turning the skewers a few times, to brown the cottage cheese evenly on all sides. Take the cottage cheese pieces off the skewers and place them on a plate and set aside to cool.

4 Combine the grilled cottage cheese, pineapple, cucumber, capsicum, roughly torn iceberg lettuce and olives in a large serving bowl. Drizzle the dressing over and toss to mix well. Serve immediately.

starters

olive all' ascolana

40 green olives, stoned

¼ cup grated processed cheese

2 tablespoons cheese spread

½ tablespoon mixed dried herbs

10 garlic cloves, chopped

1 teaspoon red chilli flakes

Salt to taste

½ cup refined flour

1 egg, beaten

½ cup breadcrumbs

Oil for deep-frying

1 Mix together the cheese, cheese spread, dried herbs, garlic, chilli flakes and salt.

2 Stuff the olives with small portions of the cheese mixture.

3 Coat the stuffed olives with refined flour, dip in beaten egg and roll in breadcrumbs. Dip once again in beaten egg and roll in breadcrumbs.

4 Heat the oil in a deep pan and deep-fry the olives until crisp and golden. Drain on absorbent paper and serve hot.

teriyaki rolls

4 medium crusty rolls

1 tablespoon olive oil

2 medium green capsicums, seeded and sliced

10 medium fresh button mushrooms, sliced

1 large onion, sliced

½ cup firm tofu cubes

Teriyaki Sauce

1 tablespoon butter

1 inch ginger, sliced

1 medium onion, finely chopped

½ cup white wine

12-15 black grapes, crushed

1 tablespoon soy sauce

½ teaspoon black pepper powder

Salt to taste

1 tablespoon molasses

2 tablespoons honey

1 To make the teriyaki sauce, heat the butter in a non-stick pan. Add the ginger and onion and sauté till golden.

2 Add the white wine and cook till the mixture reduces a little.

3 Add the crushed black grapes and continue to cook, stirring for five to seven minutes till the grapes become soft.

4 Add the soy sauce, pepper powder, salt, molasses and honey. Mix well and strain the sauce. Set it aside.

5 Heat the oil in a pan, add the capsicum, mushrooms, onion and tofu and toss for two minutes.

6 Add the teriyaki sauce and mix. Cook for two minutes. Divide the mixture into four portions.

7 Halve the crusty rolls and spread one portion of the vegetable and tofu mixture on one half of each roll and cover it with the other half.

chao tom

8 six-inch long sugarcane sticks, peeled

2 tablespoons oil

Seasoned Prawns

300 grams medium prawns, peeled and deveined

1 teaspoon salt

¼ cup minced chicken

¼ cup flaked white fish fillet

3 garlic cloves

3 shallots

1 teaspoon sugar

1 egg white, beaten

1 tablespoon fish sauce

1 tablespoon roasted rice powder

¼ teaspoon black pepper powder

To Garnish

1 head iceberg lettuce, leaves separated

80 grams rice vermicelli (optional), blanched and drained

4 shallots, sliced and crisply fried

A few sprigs of fresh coriander

A few sprigs of fresh mint

To Serve

Fish Sauce Dip (page 127)

1 For the seasoned prawns, rub salt into the prawns and set aside for fifteen minutes. Rinse and drain.

2 Grind the prawns, chicken, fish, garlic, shallots and sugar to a paste in a blender. Add the egg white, fish sauce, roasted rice powder and pepper powder, and mix well. Divide into eight equal portions.

3 Lightly grease your hands and wrap a portion of the prawn mixture tightly around the middle of a sugarcane stick. Repeat with the remaining mixture and sugarcane sticks.

4 Heat a grill pan and grill the sticks over medium heat for five to ten minutes, rotating them frequently, until lightly browned on all sides. Remove and place on a plate.

5 On individual serving plates, arrange the lettuce leaves, rice vermicelli, fried shallots, coriander and mint. Arrange the prawn sticks on top and serve with the fish sauce dip.

golden bags

30 five-inch round spring roll wrappers

1 cup crumbled cottage cheese

½ cup minced mixed vegetables (cauliflower, French beans and green peas)

1 tablespoon chopped fresh coriander

¼ teaspoon black pepper powder

Salt to taste

2 tablespoons oil + for deep-frying

10 garlic cloves, chopped

A few spring onion greens

½ cup sweet chilli sauce

1 To make the filling, mix together the cottage cheese, vegetables, chopped coriander, pepper and salt.

2 Heat two tablespoons of oil in a wok; add the garlic and sauté until fragrant. Add the cottage cheese mixture and stir-fry for three to four minutes.

3 Place one tablespoon of the filling in the centre of each spring roll sheet, and gather the edges together in pleats to make a bag *(potli)*. Tie the bag tightly around the filling with a strip of spring onion green stalk. Trim the excess wrapper and the spring onion.

4 Heat plenty of oil in a deep wok and deep-fry the bags until golden. Drain on absorbent paper.

5 Serve hot with sweet chilli sauce.

aloo nazakat

4 large potatoes
2 tablespoons oil + for deep-frying
3 teaspoons ginger-garlic paste
Salt to taste
1 cup yogurt, whisked
½ teaspoon black salt
1 teaspoon *garam masala* powder
1 teaspoon red chilli powder
3 tablespoons roasted split Bengal gram, powdered
3 tablespoons chopped fresh coriander
2 tablespoons mustard oil
½ cup grated cottage cheese
2 teaspoons *chaat masala*
2 green chillies, chopped
2 small fried *urad dal papads*, crushed

1 Peel and scoop out the insides of the potatoes leaving a shell all around. Chop the scooped out portion and set aside. Heat sufficient oil in a *kadai* and deep-fry the potato shells till cooked and the outer surface turns golden brown. Drain on absorbent paper.

2 Heat the oil in a pan and add one teaspoon of the ginger-garlic paste. Add the chopped potatoes and salt and cook over medium heat for five to six minutes.

3 For the marinade, place the yogurt in a bowl; add the salt, black salt, *garam masala* powder, chilli powder, roasted split Bengal gram powder, two tablespoons of the chopped coriander, the remaining ginger-garlic paste and mix well. Add the mustard oil and mix again. Set aside.

4 For the stuffing, place the cottage cheese in a bowl. Add the salt, the *chaat masala*, remaining chopped coriander, green chillies, cooked potatoes and crushed fried *papad*. Mix well.

5 Stuff the potato shells generously with the cottage cheese mixture. Place the stuffed potatoes into the yogurt marinade and mix well with a light hand. Leave to marinate for about thirty minutes.

6 Preheat an oven to 180°C/350°F/Gas Mark 4. Grease a baking tray.

7 Arrange the stuffed potatoes on the baking tray and bake for fifteen to twenty minutes. Serve hot.

paneer-stuffed papad rolls

8 seven-inch *urad dal papad*

150 grams cottage cheese, cut into ½-inch cubes

1-2 green chillies, chopped

½ teaspoon red chilli powder

½ teaspoon cumin powder

1 teaspoon *chaat masala*

2 tablespoons chopped fresh coriander

½ inch ginger, chopped

Salt to taste

1 Mix together the cottage cheese, green chillies, chilli powder, cumin powder, *chaat masala*, chopped coriander, ginger and salt.

2 Cut each *papad* in half. Roast directly over an open flame or on a hot *tawa* and shape immediately into a cone.

3 Arrange the cones in a deep bowl and stuff them with the cottage cheese mixture.

4 Serve immediately.

mexican chaat

25-30 tortilla or corn chips, crushed

1 cup corn kernels, boiled

2 medium potatoes, boiled and chopped

1 large onion, chopped

1 large tomato, chopped

1 jalapeño chilli, chopped

2-3 tablespoons Green Chutney (page 126)

3-4 tablespoons Date and Tamarind Chutney (page 126)

Salt to taste

1 cup yogurt, whisked and chilled

1 tablespoon chopped fresh coriander

1 In a large bowl, combine the crushed corn chips (reserving some for garnishing), corn, potatoes, onion, tomato, jalapeño chilli, two tablespoons of green chutney, three tablespoons of date and tamarind chutney and salt; toss well to mix.

2 Add the chilled yogurt and mix well with a spoon or a spatula.

3 Transfer the mixture to a platter, drizzle the remaining green chutney and date and tamarind chutney on top, and serve, garnished with the reserved corn chips and the chopped coriander.

hara bhara kabab

100 grams fresh spinach leaves, blanched and chopped

¾ cup shelled green peas, boiled and mashed

3-4 medium potatoes, boiled and grated

2 green chillies, chopped

2 tablespoons chopped fresh coriander

1 inch ginger, chopped

1 teaspoon *chaat masala*

Salt to taste

2 tablespoons cornflour

Oil for deep-frying

1 Mix together the spinach, peas and potatoes. Add the green chillies, fresh coriander, ginger, *chaat masala* and salt. Mix in the cornflour.

2 Divide the mixture into twenty-four portions. Shape each portion into a ball and then press it between your palms to make a flat *tikki*.

3 Heat sufficient oil in a *kadai*. Deep-fry the *tikki* in hot oil for three to four minutes.

4 Drain on absorbent paper and serve hot.

kachori chaat

1 cup refined flour

¼ teaspoon carom seeds

¼ teaspoon salt

A pinch of soda bicarbonate

2 tablespoons ghee

Oil for deep-frying

Filling

½ cup shelled green peas, lightly crushed

½ tablespoon oil

A pinch of asafoetida

¼ teaspoon cumin seeds

½ inch ginger, chopped

2 green chillies, chopped

Salt to taste

¼ teaspoon *garam masala* powder

2 tablespoons grated coconut

2 tablespoons roasted peanuts, crushed

Topping

2 cups yogurt, whisked and chilled

1 teaspoon red chilli powder

2 teaspoons roasted cumin powder

4 teaspoons Green Chutney (page 126)

4 teaspoons Date and Tamarind Chutney (page 126)

1 For the filling, heat the oil in a pan; add the asafoetida and cumin seeds. When the cumin seeds begin to change colour, add the ginger, green chillies, green peas and salt. Mix and cook for two or three minutes. Remove from heat and stir in the *garam masala* powder. Set aside to cool. When completely cold, add the coconut and peanuts and mix well.

2 For the *kachori*, mix together the refined flour, carom seeds, salt, soda bicarbonate and pure ghee in a bowl. Add enough cold water and knead into a stiff dough.

3 Divide the dough into eight equal portions. Roll out each portion and press to make round *puris*. Stuff each *puri* with the stuffing and shape into a *kachori*.

4 Heat plenty of oil in a *kadai* and deep-fry the *kachori* in moderately hot oil till crisp and golden. Drain on absorbent paper.

5 To serve, lightly crush two to three *kachori* and place them in individual serving bowls. Pour some yogurt over, sprinkle chilli powder and cumin powder, drizzle both the chutneys and serve immediately.

biscuit corn sev puri

16 cream cracker biscuits

½ cup corn kernels, blanched

1 cup fine *sev*

2 large potatoes, boiled and mashed

Salt to taste

¼ teaspoon red chilli powder

2 medium onions, chopped

Chaat masala, as required

8-10 teaspoons Green Chutney (page 126)

2 tablespoons Red Chilli-Garlic Chutney (page 126)

8-10 teaspoons Date and Tamarind Chutney (page 126)

2 tablespoons chopped fresh coriander

1 small unripe mango, chopped

1 Arrange four biscuits on each plate.

2 In a separate bowl, mix together the mashed potatoes, corn, salt and chilli powder. Divide into sixteen portions. Place a portion of the potato mixture on each biscuit. Sprinkle onion and *chaat masala* on top.

3 Drizzle half a teaspoon of green chutney, one-fourth teaspoon of red chilli-garlic chutney and one teaspoon of date and tamarind chutney one over the other on each biscuit. Cover the biscuits with plenty of *sev*.

4 Sprinkle fresh coriander and unripe mango on top. Serve immediately.

Chef's Tip: Add more red chilli-garlic chutney for a spicier snack.

canapés with chole

16 ready-made canapés, fried

1½ cups yogurt, whisked and chilled

1 teaspoon red chilli powder

2 teaspoons roasted cumin powder

2 teaspoons *chaat masala*

¼ cup Green Chutney (page 126)

Chole

1 cup chickpeas, soaked

Salt to taste

2 teaspoons tea leaves

2 tablespoons ghee

2 medium onions, chopped

1 teaspoon ginger paste

1 teaspoon garlic paste

4 tablespoons *chole masala*

¾ cup fresh tomato purée

4 tablespoons chopped fresh coriander

1 To make the *chole*, place the chickpeas with three cups of water and salt in a pressure cooker. Tie the tea leaves in a piece of muslin to make a *potli*; add to the chickpeas. Seal the cooker and cook till the pressure is released five to six times (five to six whistles) or till the chickpeas are soft. Discard the *potli*. Drain and set aside. Reserve one-fourth cup of stock for cooking.

2 Heat two tablespoons of ghee in a *kadai*; add the onions and sauté over low heat till light golden. Add the ginger paste and garlic paste and sauté for half a minute.

3 Add three tablespoons of *chole masala* and continue to sauté for another minute. Add the tomato purée and cook over low heat for two to three minutes.

4 Add the boiled chickpeas and the reserved stock and simmer for five minutes, or till all the water is absorbed and the ghee rises to the surface. Sprinkle the remaining *chole masala* and chopped coriander, stir and cover immediately. Remove from heat and keep warm.

5 Place the canapés on individual serving plates. Fill each canapé with two to three tablespoons of prepared *chole*. Pour some whisked yogurt over and sprinkle a little chilli powder, roasted cumin powder and *chaat masala*. Finally drizzle a little green chutney on each canapé and serve immediately.

black grape pani puri

Crisp *puri* (meant for *pani puri*), as required

1 litre fresh black grape juice

½ medium bunch (100 grams) fresh mint

¼ medium bunch (100 grams) fresh coriander

3-4 green chillies

2 tablespoons Tamarind Pulp (page 126)

Salt to taste

½ teaspoon black salt

1 teaspoon roasted cumin powder

1 teaspoon red chilli powder

1 tablespoon lemon juice

Filling Options

Sprouted green gram, as required

Potatoes, boiled and mashed, as required

1 Grind the mint, coriander and green chillies to a fine paste.

2 Mix together the black grape juice, ground paste, tamarind pulp, salt, black salt, roasted cumin powder, chilli powder and lemon juice.

3 Chill in a refrigerator till required.

4 To serve, place a little sprouted green gram or mashed potato in each *puri*, fill with the grape juice mixture and eat at once.

badami tangdi

4 (115 grams each) whole chicken legs (drumstick and thigh)

First Marinade

½ teaspoon salt

½ teaspoon red chilli powder

2-3 tablespoons lemon juice

Second Marinade

½ cup drained hung yogurt

2 tablespoons thick cream

2 tablespoons almond paste

2 teaspoons dried fenugreek leaves

2 tablespoons cornflour

2 tablespoons ginger-garlic paste

¾ teaspoon salt

2 tablespoons chopped fresh coriander

Basting Sauce

3 tablespoons melted butter

1 teaspoon white pepper powder

2 teaspoons dried fenugreek leaves

To Garnish

½ teaspoon *chaat masala*

½ tablespoon lemon juice

To Serve

A few onion rings

Mint Chutney (page 126)

1 Wash and pat the chicken legs dry. Make two incisions on each leg.

2 For the first marinade, mix together the salt, chilli powder and lemon juice; marinate the chicken legs in the mixture for half an hour.

3 For the second marinade, mix together the yogurt, cream, almond paste dried fenugreek leaves, cornflour, ginger-garlic paste, salt and chopped coriander in a bowl.

4 Remove the chicken legs from the first marinade and place them in the second marinade. Marinate for at least two to three hours, preferably in a refrigerator. You can marinate the chicken legs overnight as well.

5 Preheat the oven to 180°C/350°F/Gas Mark 4 or heat a gas *tandoo*r over medium heat for fifteen minutes.

6 Place the marinated chicken legs on the greased wire rack and cook for fifteen minutes.

7 For the basting sauce, add the white pepper powder and dried fenugreek leaves to the melted butter and mix. Turn the chicken legs once and baste with this mixture. Grill for another eight minutes, or till cooked.

8 Sprinkle some *chaat masala* and lemon juice over each chicken leg. Serve hot with onion rings and mint chutney.

Note: While threading pieces of meat or vegetable onto a skewer, leave a gap of at least one inch between pieces so that they have enough space and heat to cook thoroughly.

chicken 65

450 grams boneless chicken, cut into 1½-inch pieces

½ cup yogurt

1½ tablespoons lemon juice

2 tablespoons rice flour

Salt to taste

6 tablespoons oil

Masala

4 dried red chillies

2 inches ginger

6 garlic cloves

2 tablespoons coriander seeds

12-15 black peppercorns

1 Grind the ingredients for the *masala* to a fine paste.

2 Mix together the yogurt, lemon juice, rice flour, salt and two tablespoons oil into the ground *masala* paste.

3 Coat the chicken with the paste and marinate for an hour in a refrigerator.

4 Heat the remaining oil in a thick-bottomed *kadai*; add the chicken in small batches of six to eight pieces, and stir-fry over high heat for one minute, tossing continuously. Add another batch of the chicken and repeat.

5 Lower the heat once all the chicken has been added. Turn the pieces frequently, basting with the remaining *masala.*

6 Cook till the oil separates and the chicken turns crispy on the outside, but moist and soft on the inside.

7 Adjust salt, toss well and remove. Drain and serve hot.

fish tikka achaari

2 (400 grams), king fish fillets, cut into 2-inch pieces
2 tablespoons lemon juice
Salt to taste
1 teaspoon garlic paste
1 teaspoon ginger paste
½ teaspoon turmeric powder
2 teaspoons Kashmiri chilli powder
1 teaspoon mustard seeds, roasted
1 teaspoon fennel seeds
1 teaspoon onion seeds
½ teaspoon fenugreek seeds
½ teaspoon black salt
2 tablespoons mustard oil
1 cup yogurt, whisked
4 tablespoons butter, melted

1 Place the fish fillets in a bowl; add the lemon juice, salt, garlic paste, ginger paste, turmeric powder and chilli powder and mix well.

2 Heat a pan and dry-roast the mustard seeds, fennel seeds, onion seeds and fenugreek seeds. Crush them along with the black salt with a mortar and pestle.

3 Heat the mustard oil in a pan to smoking point. Set aside to cool.

4 Add the yogurt along with the crushed spices and mix. Leave to stand for thirty minutes.

5 Preheat an oven to 220°C/425°F/Gas Mark 7.

6 Add the cooled mustard oil to the marinated fish and mix.

7 Place the fish on a greased rack over a tray in the preheated oven. Cook, for ten to fifteen minutes or till tender, basting with butter once while cooking.

8 Serve hot.

Chef's Note:
If you do not have an oven, you can thread the pieces of fish onto a skewer and cook them on a hot non-stick *tawa*.

kasoori jhinga

2 tablespoons powdered dried fenugreek leaves
20 (300 grams) medium prawns
2 tablespoons ginger-garlic paste
2 tablespoons lemon juice
Salt to taste
10 curry leaves
1 cup fresh coriander
¼ cup fresh mint
3 green chillies
1 cup drained (hung) yogurt
3 tablespoons fresh cream
1 egg
2 teaspoons Kashmiri chilli powder
½ teaspoon carom seeds
½ teaspoon *garam masala* powder
2 tablespoons cornflour
3 tablespoons oil
Melted butter for basting

1 Peel and devein the prawns leaving the tails intact. Mix together one tablespoon dried fenugreek leaves, one tablespoon ginger-garlic paste, the lemon juice and salt in a bowl and rub the mixture over the prawns. Set aside for half an hour.

2 Grind together the curry leaves, fresh coriander, fresh mint and green chillies to a fine paste. Transfer to a deep bowl. Add the yogurt, remaining ginger-garlic paste, salt, fresh cream, egg, chilli powder, carom seeds, *garam masala* powder, cornflour, oil and the remaining dried fenugreek leaves.

3 Squeeze out the excess moisture from the marinated prawns and add to the yogurt mixture and mix well. Set aside for an hour, preferably in a refrigerator.

4 Preheat the oven to 200°C/400°F/Gas Mark 6.

5 Thread the prawns onto skewers leaving a little distance between each one. Drizzle the remaining marinade over the prawns.

6 Cook in the preheated oven for three to five minutes, basting with butter once while cooking.

7 Serve hot with onion rings and lemon wedges.

dum ke kabab

450 grams minced mutton

½ tablespoon unripe green papaya paste

Oil for deep-frying

2 medium onions, sliced

1 inch cinnamon

4 green cardamoms

3 cloves

½ teaspoon allspice

1 teaspoon cudpah nuts

½ teaspoon poppy seeds

1 tablespoon grated dried coconut

3 dried red chillies, broken into pieces

½ teaspoon caraway seeds

3 green chillies

2 tablespoons chopped fresh coriander

3-4 garlic cloves

½ inch ginger

1½ teaspoons gram flour

¾ cup yogurt, whisked

¼ cup cream

1 tablespoon lemon juice

Salt to taste

A pinch of red chilli powder

A pinch of *garam masala* powder

1½ tablespoons pure ghee

To Garnish

1 medium onion, cut into rings

A few fresh mint sprigs

1 lemon, cut into wedges

1 Mix the green papaya paste into the minced mutton and leave to marinate for fifteen minutes. Grind till smooth.

2 Heat the oil in a *kadai* and deep-fry the onions till golden. Drain on absorbent paper.

3 Dry-roast the cinnamon, cardamoms, cloves and allspice separately till fragrant. Cool and grind to a fine powder.

4 Dry-roast the cudpah nuts, poppy seeds, dried coconut, red chillies and caraway seeds separately till fragrant. Grind the spices together with the green chillies, fresh coriander, garlic and ginger to a smooth paste. Roast the gram flour over a low heat till fragrant. Mix all the above ingredients with the minced mutton and grind twice. Add half a cup of yogurt, the cream, lemon juice and salt. Cover and place the mixture in the refrigerator for thirty minutes.

5 Preheat an oven to 220°C/425°F/Gas Mark 7.

6 Divide the chilled mixture into twenty-four equal portions and shape into balls. Grease your palms with a little oil and shape the balls into sausages. Arrange on a greased tray and set aside.

7 Place the remaining yogurt in a small bowl; add a pinch each of chilli powder and *garam masala* powder and whisk thoroughly. Spoon a little of this mixture onto each kabab. Cook in the oven for twenty minutes, basting now and then with ghee.

8 Remove from the oven and serve hot with onion rings, fresh mint and lemon wedges.

vegetable tempura

8 medium cauliflower florets

1 medium green capsicum, cut into 1-inch triangles

1 medium red capsicum, cut into 1-inch triangles

1 medium yellow capsicum, cut into 1-inch triangles

1 medium carrot, cut into thin round slices

1 medium onion, cut into 1-inch cubes, layers separated

½ teaspoon white pepper powder

Salt to taste

¾ cup refined flour

½ cup cornflour

¼ teaspoon baking powder

¾ cup oil + for deep-frying

1 Place all the vegetables in a bowl. Add the white pepper powder and salt and toss well. Place in a refrigerator to chill for about fifteen minutes.

2 Mix together the flour, cornflour, baking powder, three-fourth cup oil, salt to taste and three-fourth cup of chilled water. Whisk thoroughly to make a batter of pouring consistency. Set aside for twenty minutes.

3 Heat the oil in a wok. Dip the vegetables, one by one, in the batter and deep-fry over medium heat, turning frequently or until crisp and golden brown. Drain on absorbent paper.

4 Serve hot with sauce.

Chef's Tip:

For a crisper result, increase the quantity of oil in the batter. Whisk well to incorporate the oil thoroughly.

phal-subz seekh

2 unripe bananas

2 medium potatoes, boiled and mashed

200 grams fresh button mushrooms, chopped

1 small carrot, grated

4 broccoli florets, chopped

1½ tablespoons butter

¾ teaspoon carom seeds

¾ tablespoon chopped fresh coriander

¾ inch ginger, chopped

1½ fresh red chillies, chopped

Salt to taste

12 prunes, chopped

½ teaspoon black salt

¾ teaspoon black pepper powder

½ teaspoon green cardamom powder

A pinch of sandalwood powder

A pinch of dried rose petal powder

½ cup breadcrumbs

1½ tablespoons oil

1 Boil, cool, peel and grate the bananas.

2 Heat the butter in a pan; add the carom seeds and sauté over medium heat for ten seconds. Add the mushrooms, carrot and broccoli and sauté till the moisture evaporates. Add the chopped coriander, ginger, red chillies and salt. Stir and remove from heat and set aside to cool.

3 Place the cooled mixture in a blender with the grated bananas, prunes, black salt, pepper powder, cardamom powder, sandalwood powder, rose petal powder, and breadcrumbs and process till smooth.

4 Transfer the mixture to a bowl and divide into equal portions.

5 Pat the mixture onto skewers into four-inch long *seekh* kabab.

6 Preheat a *tandoor*. Cook the kabab in the *tandoor* for six or seven minutes, basting occasionally with oil.

7 Alternatively, shape each portion into a croquette, arrange on a greased baking tray and grill in a preheated oven at 180°C/350°F/Gas Mark 4 for six or seven minutes.

8 Arrange the kabab on a platter and serve hot with *Kachumber* (page 126).

veg main courses

achaari gobhi

1 medium cauliflower

3 tablespoons mustard oil

½ teaspoon mustard seeds

½ teaspoon cumin seeds

¼ teaspoon fenugreek seeds

½ teaspoon fennel seeds

¼ teaspoon onion seeds

1 teaspoon coriander seeds, crushed

¼ teaspoon asafoetida

1 medium onion, chopped

1 teaspoon ginger paste

1 teaspoon garlic paste

3 green chillies, chopped

Salt to taste

½ teaspoon turmeric power

¾ cup yogurt

1 Separate the cauliflower into large florets.

2 Heat the mustard oil to smoking point in a *kadai*; add the mustard seeds, cumin seeds, fenugreek seeds, fennel seeds, onion seeds, crushed coriander seeds and asafoetida, and sauté till they begin to change colour.

3 Add the onion and sauté till translucent. Add the ginger paste, garlic paste and green chillies and sauté till the onion turns light brown.

4 Add the cauliflower and salt and sauté over medium heat till brown.

5 Add the turmeric powder and one cup of water and cook, covered, for ten to fifteen minutes, or till cooked.

6 Add the yogurt and continue to cook till the water evaporates and the gravy coats the cauliflower. Serve hot.

capsicum kayras

5-6 medium green capsicums, cut into 1-inch pieces

2 medium potatoes, cut into 1-inch cubes

½ cup raw peanuts

1 tablespoon oil

½ teaspoon mustard seeds

A pinch of asafoetida

¼ teaspoon turmeric powder

Salt to taste

1½ tablespoons grated jaggery

Masala

½ cup grated coconut

3 tablespoons sesame seeds

½ tablespoon oil

2 tablespoons split Bengal gram

2 tablespoons coriander seeds

¼ teaspoon fenugreek seeds

4-5 dried Bedgi red chillies

2 tablespoons Tamarind Pulp (page 126)

1 For the *masala*, separately dry-roast the coconut and sesame seeds in a pan till fragrant and lightly coloured. Transfer to a plate and set aside to cool.

2 Heat half a tablespoon of oil in the same pan; add the split Bengal gram, coriander seeds, fenugreek seeds and red chillies and sauté till fragrant. Grind along with the roasted coconut and sesame seeds, and the tamarind pulp to a fine paste with three-fourth cup of water.

3 Heat the oil in a pan; add the mustard seeds and when they begin to splutter, add the asafoetida. Add the peanuts and sauté for three to four minutes.

4 Add the potatoes, turmeric powder, salt and jaggery. Stir, cover and cook over low heat for five minutes. Add the capsicum, stir and cook till the vegetables are partially cooked.

5 Add the ground paste and one and a half cups of water, and cook over low heat for three to four minutes. Serve hot.

methi-baingan

2 bunches (500 grams) fresh fenugreek leaves, chopped

10-12 small brinjals

Salt to taste

2 teaspoons red chilli powder

½ teaspoon dried mango powder

2 tablespoons oil

½ teaspoon mustard seeds

8-10 curry leaves

1 green chilli, chopped

2 medium onions, chopped

1½ tablespoons ginger-garlic paste

2 medium tomatoes, chopped

1 teaspoon cumin powder

1 teaspoon coriander powder

½ teaspoon turmeric powder

½ teaspoon *garam masala* powder

2 tablespoons chopped fresh coriander

1 Slit the brinjals lengthways into four keeping the stem intact.

2 Rub the salt, one teaspoon of chilli powder and the dried mango powder into the slit brinjals and set aside.

3 Heat the oil in a pressure cooker; add the mustard seeds. When they begin to splutter, add the curry leaves, green chilli and onions and sauté till the onions turn golden.

4 Add the ginger-garlic paste and continue to sauté for one minute. Stir in the chopped tomato, remaining chilli powder, cumin powder and coriander powder. Add the turmeric powder, *garam masala* powder and half a cup of water and bring the mixture to a boil.

5 Add the brinjals, fenugreek leaves and salt. Seal the cooker with the lid and cook till the pressure is released once (one whistle). Lower the heat and cook for two minutes.

6 Take the cooker off the heat and remove the lid when the pressure has reduced completely. Garnish with chopped coriander and serve hot.

dahi papad ki sabzi

1½ cups sour yogurt

3 *Bikaneri moong papad*

¾ tablespoon gram flour

½ teaspoon turmeric powder

¾ teaspoon red chilli powder

Salt to taste

2½ tablespoons pure ghee

1 teaspoon cumin seeds

1½ teaspoons coriander powder

½ teaspoon asafoetida

2 dried red chillies, broken into large bits

¾ cup *boondi*

1 tablespoon chopped fresh coriander

½ teaspoon *garam masala* powder

1 In a large bowl, combine the yogurt, gram flour, turmeric powder, chilli powder and salt. Add two cups of water and mix well. Strain and set aside.

2 Heat the ghee in a *kadai* and add the cumin seeds. When they change colour, add the coriander powder and sauté for one minute.

3 Add the asafoetida and red chillies, and sauté for half a minute.

4 Add the yogurt mixture and adjust the seasoning. Stir continuously till the mixture comes to a boil. Lower the heat and simmer for two minutes.

5 Heat a *tawa* and roast the *papad* on both sides. Break each one roughly into two-inch pieces.

6 Add the *papad* and *boondi* to the simmering yogurt mixture and cook for two or three minutes.

7 Garnish with the chopped coriander and *garam masala* powder. Serve hot.

shahi paneer

400 grams skimmed milk cottage cheese
2 large onions, quartered
1 tablespoon oil
3 cloves
4-5 black peppercorns
2 one-inch sticks cinnamon
1 bay leaf
2 green chillies, slit
1 teaspoon ginger paste
1 teaspoon garlic paste
1 tablespoon cashew nut paste
2 tablespoons melon seed paste
½ cup yogurt
½ cup cream
A pinch of saffron
½ teaspoon *garam masala* powder
Salt to taste
¼ teaspoon green cardamom powder

1 Cut the cottage cheese into half-inch wide and one-inch long pieces.

2 Boil the onions in quarter cup of water. Drain and allow it to cool. Grind to a fine paste.

3 Heat the oil in a non-stick *kadai*, add the cloves, black peppercorns, cinnamon and bay leaf and sauté till fragrant. Add the green chillies and boiled onion paste and sauté for three to four minutes on low heat so that it retains its colour.

4 Add the ginger paste and garlic paste and continue to sauté for half a minute. Add the cashew nut paste and melon seed paste and sauté for a further two minutes.

5 Add the yogurt and sauté till the water from the yogurt is absorbed. Add the cream, saffron and *garam masala* powder and stir. Add salt to taste.

6 Add the cottage cheese and stir gently. Sprinkle the cardamom powder and serve hot.

paneer khurchan

250 grams cottage cheese, cut into thick strips
2 tablespoons oil
1 teaspoon cumin seeds
2 teaspoons garlic paste
2 medium green capsicums, cut into thick strips
2 medium tomatoes, seeded and cut into thick strips
2 medium onions, cut into thick strips
3 tablespoons tomato purée
Salt to taste
1 teaspoon red chilli powder
1 teaspoon lemon juice
1 teaspoon dried fenugreek leaves, roasted and crushed

1 Heat the oil in a thick-bottomed *kadai*; add the cumin seeds. When they begin to change colour, add the garlic paste, capsicums, tomatoes and onions, and sauté for five or six minutes.

2 Add the cottage cheese, tomato purée, salt and chilli powder. Sauté for a while till the cottage cheese begins to stick to the pan.

3 Scrape the cottage cheese off the bottom of the pan and sauté for a while longer till the cottage cheese is dark brown and mashed.

4 Stir in the lemon juice and dried fenugreek leaves, and serve immediately.

ekadashi jeera aloo

500 grams baby potatoes, parboiled and halved
1 teaspoon cumin seeds
4 tablespoons oil
15-18 curry leaves
2 green chillies, slit
Rock salt to taste
1½ teaspoons sugar
2 tablespoons lemon juice
2 tablespoons chopped fresh coriander
3 tablespoons grated coconut

1 Heat the oil in a *kadai*; add the cumin seeds, curry leaves and green chillies and sauté till they begin to change colour.

2 Add the potatoes and rock salt and sauté over medium heat for two minutes. Cover and cook over low heat till the potatoes are completely done and well browned.

3 Add the sugar, lemon juice, chopped coriander and coconut. Toss well to mix. Serve hot.

Ekadashi Jeera Aloo

paneer tamatar ka khut

250 grams cottage cheese

8-10 medium tomatoes, chopped

½ lemon-sized ball tamarind

2 one-inch pieces ginger, chopped

10-12 garlic cloves, crushed

6-8 dried red chillies, broken into large bits

1 tablespoon sesame oil

1 teaspoon mustard seeds

1 teaspoon cumin seeds

20 curry leaves

3 one-inch cinnamon sticks

1 teaspoon turmeric powder

2 teaspoons coriander powder

1 teaspoon roasted cumin powder

Salt to taste

¼ cup roasted split Bengal gram, powdered

¼ cup Coconut Milk (page 126)

1 Cut the cottage cheese into fingers. Soak the tamarind in half a cup of warm water for half an hour; squeeze out the pulp, strain and set aside.

2 Heat half a cup of water in a pan; add the tomatoes, ginger, garlic and red chillies and bring to a boil. Lower heat, cover and simmer for fifteen to twenty minutes, or till the gravy is reduced to half the original quantity. Remove from heat and set aside to cool. Pass the cooled mixture through a fine mesh or a soup strainer.

3 Heat the sesame oil in a pan; add the mustard seeds and cumin seeds and sauté until the mustard seeds begin to splutter. Add the curry leaves, cinnamon, turmeric powder, coriander powder and cumin powder and sauté for one minute.

4 Add the strained tomato mixture and bring to a boil. Stir in the tamarind pulp and salt. Add the powdered roasted Bengal gram and mix thoroughly. Lower the heat and stir in the coconut milk and cottage cheese. Simmer for two or three minutes and serve hot.

baghare baingan

250 grams small brinjals
2 medium onions, quartered
1½ teaspoons coriander seeds
1½ tablespoons sesame seeds
2 tablespoons peanuts
½ teaspoon cumin seeds
¾ teaspoon poppy seeds
1 tablespoon grated dried coconut
A pinch of fenugreek seeds
1 inch ginger, chopped
6-8 garlic cloves, chopped
Salt to taste
A pinch of turmeric power
½ teaspoon red chilli powder
½ teaspoon grated jaggery or sugar
2 tablespoons Tamarind Pulp (page 126)
½ cup oil
A sprig of curry leaves

1 Wash the brinjals and slit lengthways into four, with the quarters held together at the stalk end.

2 Dry-roast the onions on a *tawa* till soft and pale gold. Dry-roast the coriander seeds, sesame seeds, peanuts, cumin seeds, poppy seeds, dried coconut and fenugreek seeds all together till fragrant and they begin to change colour.

3 Grind together the roasted onions, roasted spices, ginger, garlic, salt, turmeric powder, chilli powder and jaggery to a very fine paste. Add the tamarind pulp and mix well. Stuff the slit brinjals with some *masala* and reserve the rest.

4 Heat the oil in a *kadai*; add the curry leaves and sauté for one minute. Add the stuffed brinjals and sauté for about ten minutes. Add the reserved *masala* and mix gently. Add two cups of water, cover and cook over low heat till the brinjals are completely cooked and the oil rises to the surface. Serve hot.

mirchi ka salan

18-20 large green chillies
2 tablespoons oil + for deep-frying
2 tablespoons sesame seeds
1 tablespoon coriander seeds
1 teaspoon cumin seeds
½ cup roasted peanuts
2 dried red chillies, broken into bits
1 inch ginger, chopped
6-8 garlic cloves
1 teaspoon mustard seeds
8-10 curry leaves
1 medium onion, grated
1 teaspoon turmeric powder
2 tablespoons Tamarind Pulp (page 126)
Salt to taste

1 Wash, wipe and slit the green chillies lengthways without separating into two. Heat the oil in a *kadai* and deep-fry the chillies for one minute. Drain on absorbent paper and set aside.

2 Dry-roast the sesame seeds, coriander seeds and cumin seeds. Cool and grind to a paste along with the peanuts, red chillies, ginger and garlic.

3 Heat two tablespoons of oil in a pan and add the mustard seeds. When they begin to splutter add the curry leaves and sauté for half a minute. Add the onion and sauté, stirring continuously, till light golden brown.

4 Add the turmeric powder and mix well. Add the *masala* paste and cook for three minutes, stirring continuously. Stir in one and a half cups of water and bring to a boil. Lower the heat and cook for ten minutes. Stir in the tamarind pulp (mix the pulp with half a cup of water, if it is too thick). Add the fried green chillies and salt and cook over a low heat for eight to ten minutes. Serve hot.

Note: In Hyderabad, *Mirchi ka Salan* is traditionally served as an accompaniment to *biryani*. Some people like to add grated coconut to the *masala* paste, but I prefer it without the coconut. The gravy is also referred to as *Tili* (*til*=sesame) *aur Falli* (*Moongfalli*=peanuts) gravy.

khumb hara dhania

600 grams fresh button mushrooms, trimmed
1 cup chopped fresh coriander
2 tablespoons oil
5 green cardamoms
1 black cardamom
5 cloves
1 inch cinnamon
1 bay leaf
A pinch of mace
⅔ cup boiled onion paste
4 teaspoons ginger paste
4 teaspoons garlic paste
4 green chillies, chopped
1 teaspoon red chilli powder
½ teaspoon coriander powder
1½ cups yogurt, whisked
Salt to taste
3 tablespoons cashew nut paste
1½ inches ginger, cut into thin strips

1 Blanch the mushrooms in hot water for two minutes. Drain.

2 Heat the oil in a *kadai*; add the green and black cardamoms, cloves, cinnamon, bay leaf and mace and sauté over medium heat till fragrant.

3 Add the boiled onion paste and sauté for two or three minutes. Add the ginger and garlic pastes and continue to sauté for a while. Add the green chillies and sauté for half a minute.

4 Add the chilli powder and coriander powder and sauté for half a minute.

5 Remove from heat and stir in the yogurt and salt. Return the pan to the heat. Add around three-fourth cup of water and bring to a boil. Lower the heat and simmer till the oil rises to the surface. Add the cashew nut paste and simmer for two to three minutes.

6 Add the mushrooms and three-fourth cup of chopped coriander and simmer for two to three minutes. Transfer to a serving dish and garnish with the remaining chopped coriander and ginger strips.

7 Serve hot with steamed rice or *roti*.

shanghai stewed noodles

200 grams noodles

1 tablespoon oil

6-8 garlic cloves, crushed

1 medium onion, sliced

1 spring onion with greens, sliced

½ medium carrot, halved and sliced

4 fresh button mushrooms, sliced

¼ small cabbage, cut into 1-inch pieces

½ medium green capsicum, cut into 1-inch pieces

5 cups Vegetable Stock (page 126)

1½ tablespoons cornflour

¼ teaspoon MSG (optional)

½ teaspoon white pepper powder

Salt to taste

1 spring onion green stalk, sliced

2 tablespoons Chilli Oil (page 127)

1 Heat the oil in a wok; add the garlic, onion and spring onion and stir-fry for a few minutes. Add the carrot, mushrooms, cabbage and capsicum and continue to stir-fry for a minute.

2 Add the vegetable stock, bring to a boil and add the noodles. Cook over high heat for two minutes. Lower the heat and simmer for four to five minutes, or until the noodles are almost cooked.

3 Mix the cornflour with half a cup of water and add to the noodles. Stir in the MSG, white pepper powder and salt to taste. Cook, stirring frequently, over medium heat for a couple of minutes until the sauce thickens.

4 Add the sliced spring onion greens, drizzle the chilli oil and serve hot.

thai green curry with vegetables

1 medium carrot, cut into diamond shapes

½ small cauliflower, separated into small florets

2-3 baby brinjals

1 medium potato, diced

5 lemon grass stalks

2 tablespoons oil

1 teaspoon lemon juice

Salt to taste

¾ cup fresh Coconut Milk (page 126)

2-3 fresh basil leaves

Green Curry Paste

10 green chillies

3 shallots

9 garlic cloves

1 inch galangal

3-inch lemon grass stalk

¼ teaspoon grated lemon rind

A small bunch of coriander roots

2 teaspoons coriander seeds

2 teaspoons cumin seeds

Salt to taste

1 To make the green curry paste, grind together the green chillies, shallots, garlic, galangal, lemon grass, lemon rind, coriander roots, coriander seeds, cumin seeds and salt to a fine paste.

2 Blanch all the vegetables in boiling water. Tie the lemon grass in a piece of muslin. Crush it lightly.

3 Heat the oil in a non-stick pan; add the green curry paste and sauté for one minute. Add the blanched vegetables and lemon juice and cook for three to four minutes, stirring continuously. Add three cups of water and continue to cook for a few minutes.

4 Add the lemon grass bundle and cook for three to four minutes till the curry absorbs its flavour. Remove the lemon grass and discard.

5 Add the salt and coconut milk and simmer for one minute.

6 Add the basil leaves and remove from heat. Serve hot.

oodles of noodles

200 grams noodles

Salt to taste

1 tablespoon oil

2 spring onions, sliced

1 small yellow capsicum, sliced

1 small red capsicum, sliced

4-5 French beans, sliced diagonally and blanched

½ cup sweet corn kernels, boiled

2 teaspoons soy sauce

2 tablespoons hot and sweet tomato ketchup

1 tablespoon sweet chilli sauce

¼ cup bean sprouts

2 stalks spring onion greens, sliced

1 Boil the noodles in plenty of salted water. Drain, refresh in cold water and set aside.

2 Heat the oil in a pan; add the spring onions and stir-fry for a while. Add the capsicums and French beans and stir-fry for a few minutes.

3 Add the sweet corn and soy sauce and mix well. Add the noodles and salt and toss to mix.

4 Add the hot and sweet tomato ketchup and sweet chilli sauce and mix gently.

5 Add the bean sprouts and spring onion greens and mix well. Serve hot.

vegetable massaman curry

6-8 broccoli florets

1 medium red capsicum , cut into 1-inch pieces

1 medium green capsicum, cut into 1-inch pieces

1 medium yellow capsicum, cut into 1-inch pieces

3 tablespoons Massaman Curry Paste (page 127)

1 tablespoon oil

1 tablespoon soy sauce

1 tablespoon lemon juice

2 tablespoons roasted peanuts

Salt to taste

1 Heat the oil in a pan; add the vegetables and sauté for five to six minutes.

2 Stir in the soy sauce, lemon juice and roasted peanuts.

3 Add the curry paste and salt to taste and mix well.

4 Cook for another fifteen minutes and serve hot.

thai-style barbecued vegetables

8 small onions
4 zucchini
1 red capsicum
1 yellow capsicum
1 green capsicum
8 fresh button mushrooms
1 medium carrot

Marinade

7-8 garlic cloves, chopped
Salt to taste
3 teaspoons light soy sauce
2 tablespoons lemon juice
½ cup chopped fresh coriander

1 Chop all the vegetables into one-and-a-half-inch chunks.

2 Mix together all the ingredients for the marinade.

3 Mix the marinade into the vegetables and leave to marinate for at least thirty minutes.

4 Thread the vegetables onto skewers and cook over a barbecue or grill, turning at regular intervals, till nicely browned. Serve hot.

penne arrabbiata

250 grams penne (nib-shaped pasta)
5 medium tomatoes
Salt to taste
6 garlic cloves, peeled and crushed
2 medium onions, peeled and sliced
1 teaspoon crushed red chillies
1 tablespoon oregano
5-6 basil leaves, roughly torn

1 Blanch the tomatoes, peel, remove seeds and chop coarsely.

2 Cook the penne in plenty of boiling salted water, drain, refresh in cold water and set aside.

3 Heat a non-stick pan; add the garlic and cook until light brown.

4 Add the onions and cook till translucent. Add the crushed red chillies, oregano and tomatoes.

5 Cook for about five minutes over low heat. Add the salt and mix well.

6 Add the cooked penne and basil leaves and toss lightly. Serve hot.

vegetable stew with garlic bread

2 medium carrots, cut into 1-inch pieces

¼ small cauliflower, separated into florets

¼ cup green peas, shelled

2 medium potatoes, cut into 1-inch pieces

1 celery stalk, cut into 1-inch pieces

1 medium zucchini, cut into 1-inch pieces

¼ medium bunch (100 grams) spinach, shredded

1 inch ginger, sliced

3-4 cloves

8-10 peppercorns

1 teaspoon cumin seeds

1 medium onion, sliced

4 cups Vegetable Stock (page 126)

Salt to taste

¼ teaspoon peppercorns, crushed

1 loaf garlic bread, sliced

1 Blanch the carrots, cauliflower and green peas individually in boiling water. Refresh and set aside.

2 Tie the ginger, cloves, peppercorns and cumin seeds in a piece of muslin to make a *bouquet garni*.

3 Heat a non-stick pan. Add the onion and roast it lightly. Add the vegetable stock and bring to a boil. Add the *bouquet garni*, salt and the potatoes. Cover and cook over medium heat till the potatoes are cooked.

4 Remove the *bouquet garni* and mash the potatoes so that it thickens the stock.

5 Add the celery, zucchini, carrots, cauliflower, green peas and cook on low heat for two minutes. Adjust the salt and add the crushed peppercorns.

6 Add the spinach and mix.

7 Lightly toast the slices of garlic bread and serve with the hot stew.

pan-fried mushrooms

20-24 fresh button mushrooms, quartered

½ cup porcini mushrooms (optional)

½ cup oyster mushrooms (optional)

1 small red capsicum, seeded and cut into ½-inch pieces

1 small yellow capsicum, seeded and cut into ½-inch pieces

1 tablespoon olive oil

2 medium onions, cut into ½-inch cubes

3 garlic cloves, crushed

1 tablespoon soy sauce

1 tablespoon red chilli sauce

½ tablespoon vinegar

½ teaspoon dried thyme

Salt to taste

8-10 black peppercorns, crushed

7-8 fresh basil leaves, torn

1 If using porcini and oyster mushrooms, soak them in lukewarm water for twenty minutes. Drain. Wash well and set aside.

2 Heat the oil in a large non-stick pan. Add the onions and sauté over medium heat. When they turn translucent, add the garlic and stir-fry for a minute.

3 Add the mushrooms and the red and yellow capsicums and sauté on high heat for three minutes.

4 Add the soy sauce, chilli sauce and vinegar and sauté for a further two minutes.

5 Add the thyme, salt and crushed peppercorns.

6 Remove from heat, stir in the basil leaves and serve hot.

non-veg main courses

rendang

700 grams boneless lean mutton

2 medium onions, sliced

4 garlic cloves, crushed

1 inch galangal, sliced

1 inch ginger, sliced

4-6 fresh red chillies, seeded and sliced

1 inch lemon grass stalk, bruised and sliced

1 inch fresh turmeric, sliced
(or 1 teaspoon turmeric powder)

1 teaspoon coriander seeds, roasted and powdered

1 teaspoon cumin seeds, roasted and powdered

2 kaffir lime leaves

2 cups Coconut Milk (page 126)

1 teaspoon Tamarind Pulp (page 126) diluted in
4 tablespoons water

2 tablespoons dark soy sauce

Salt to taste

8 small potatoes

1 large onion, sliced and sautéed till browned

1 Cut the mutton into long strips and then into smaller pieces. Place them in a bowl.

2 Grind together the onions, garlic, galangal, ginger, red chillies, lemon grass and turmeric to a fine paste.

3 Add the paste to the mutton along with the roasted coriander and cumin powders and mix well. Tear the kaffir lime leaves roughly and add. Cover and leave in a cool place to marinate for half-an-hour.

4 Heat the coconut milk, three and a half cups water and tamarind water in a deep wok. Add the marinated mutton pieces and dark soy sauce and salt. Mix and bring the mixture to a boil. Lower the heat and simmer gently, half covered, for about one and a half to two hours or until the mutton is tender and the gravy thickens.

5 Add the potatoes and continue to cook. Add some more water if necessary and cook till the potatoes are tender.

6 Adjust the seasoning, and transfer into a serving bowl. Serve, garnished with the sautéed onion.

garlic-chilli crabs

2 large (200 grams each) crabs

2 tablespoons cornflour

4 tablespoons oil

14-16 garlic cloves, crushed

3-4 dried red chillies, broken in half

2 tablespoons red chilli paste

1 tablespoon soy sauce

1 teaspoon sugar

¼ teaspoon MSG (optional)

1½ cups Fish or Chicken Stock (page 126)

½ teaspoon black peppercorns crushed

Salt to taste

2 tablespoons dry sherry (optional)

1 tablespoon vinegar

2 tablespoons sesame oil

2 spring onion greens, chopped

1 Separate the claws and cut each crab into four pieces. Wash and remove the gills and stomach sac. Crack the claws lightly, wash thoroughly and drain well.

2 Mix the cornflour with half a cup of water.

3 Heat the oil in a wok or pan; add the crushed garlic and red chillies and stir-fry for a few seconds. Add the red chilli paste, soy sauce, sugar, MSG and the crab. Continue to stir-fry for two or three minutes.

4 Stir in the stock and cook for two minutes, or until the crabs are cooked.

5 Stir in the cornflour mixture and cook for one minute, or until the sauce thickens. Add the crushed peppercorns, salt, sherry and vinegar.

6 Drizzle the sesame oil and serve hot, garnished with the chopped spring onion greens.

Chef's Tip: Buy fresh crabs and have them cut and cleaned by your fishmonger, as it can be very messy to cut crabs in your kitchen.

stir-fried chicken with chillies and basil

600 grams boneless chicken, cut into thin strips

6 fresh red chillies

40 fresh basil leaves

2½ tablespoons cornflour

1 egg, beaten

Salt to taste

¼ teaspoon white pepper powder

5 tablespoons oil

6 garlic cloves, sliced

3 tablespoons fish sauce

3 teaspoons dark soy sauce

1½ teaspoons sugar

1 Slice four red chillies, remove the seeds and chop. Slice the remaining two and set aside.

2 Add the cornflour, egg, salt and white pepper powder to the chicken and mix well.

3 Heat the oil in a non-stick wok and sauté thirty basil leaves. Drain on absorbent paper and set aside.

4 In the same oil, stir-fry the marinated chicken on medium heat until crisp. Drain on absorbent paper and set aside.

5 To the same oil, add the garlic and chopped red chillies and stir-fry for half a minute or until golden.

6 Add the chicken, fish sauce, dark soy sauce and sugar and stir-fry for three to four minutes or until cooked.

7 Add the remaining basil leaves and mix.

8 Serve hot garnished with sliced red chillies and fried basil leaves.

chicken laksa

500 grams boneless chicken, cut into thin strips
1 inch ginger
3-4 garlic cloves
4 shallots
1 two-inch lemon grass stalk, bruised and chopped
3 tablespoons sesame oil
3 cups Chicken Stock (page 126)
2 fresh red chillies, seeded and sliced
1 teaspoon curry powder
100 grams snow peas, trimmed
Salt to taste
Black pepper powder to taste
1 tablespoon lemon juice
½ cup Coconut Milk (page 126)
1 cup boiled noodles
2-3 spring onions, shredded
1 medium unpeeled cucumber, sliced
1 tablespoon chopped fresh coriander
1 tablespoon chopped fresh mint
2 lemons, halved

1 Grind the ginger, garlic, shallots and lemon grass to a paste.

2 Heat two tablespoons of sesame oil in a large frying pan or wok and cook the chicken over high heat until golden brown. Drain on absorbent paper.

3 In the same pan, heat the remaining oil; add the ground paste and sauté till fragrant.

4 Add the chicken stock, red chilli slices and mix. Add the curry powder and snow peas, salt and pepper and mix again.

5 Stir in the lemon juice and coconut milk and bring to a boil.

6 To serve, place the boiled noodles in individual serving bowls and add the chicken, spring onions, cucumber, chopped fresh coriander and mint.

7 Pour the hot soup over the ingredients, fix half a lemon on the rim of the bowl and serve immediately.

braised lamb with spinach and leeks

400 grams boneless lamb, cut into ½-inch thick slices

20 spinach leaves, stems removed

1 medium leek, sliced

2 tablespoons light soy sauce

2 tablespoons fish sauce

3 tablespoons oil

½ cup chopped fresh coriander

15-20 black peppercorns, crushed

2 garlic cloves, crushed

1 tablespoon brown sugar

Salt to taste

3 tablespoons lemon juice

1 Place the lamb slices in a bowl; add the soy sauce, fish sauce, one tablespoon of oil, fresh coriander, crushed peppercorns, garlic, brown sugar and salt. Mix well and marinate the lamb for one hour in a refrigerator.

2 Drain the lamb and reserve the marinade.

3 Heat one tablespoon of oil in a wok; add the lamb slices and stir-fry for five minutes.

4 Add one cup of water and cover the wok with a lid. Cook the lamb over high heat till dry. Remove the lamb slices from the wok and keep warm.

5 Heat the remaining oil in the same wok; add the leek and stir-fry for two minutes.

6 Add the spinach leaves and cook for another thirty seconds. Add the leftover marinade and half a cup of water.

7 Bring to a boil, lower heat and simmer for five minutes; adjust seasoning.

8 Pour the sauce over the lamb, drizzle with lemon juice and serve immediately.

pan-fried pomfret in hot black bean sauce

4 (400 grams) pomfret fillets

Salt to taste

2 tablespoons malt vinegar

2 tablespoons dark soy sauce

4 tablespoons cornflour

3 tablespoons oil

2 spring onions, sliced

1 inch ginger, chopped

2 tablespoons oyster sauce

2 tablespoons hot black bean sauce

7-8 black peppercorns, crushed

1 fresh red chilli, chopped

1 teaspoon sugar

1 cup Fish or Chicken Stock (page 126)

2 stalks spring onion greens, chopped

1 Mix the salt, one tablespoon malt vinegar, one tablespoon dark soy sauce and three tablespoons cornflour in a bowl. Rub the mixture evenly over the pomfret fillets.

2 Heat two tablespoons oil in a non-stick pan and sauté the fillets for about a minute or till well done. Drain.

3 Heat the remaining oil in another non-stick pan. Add the spring onions, ginger, oyster sauce, hot black bean sauce and the remaining dark soy sauce and mix. Add the peppercorns, red chilli, sugar and stock.

4 Mix the remaining cornflour and malt vinegar in a quarter cup of water. Stir into the sauce and cook till the sauce thickens.

5 Place the fried fish on a serving plate and pour the sauce over.

6 Garnish with the spring onion greens and serve hot.

chicken curry

1 medium chicken (800 grams)

½ teaspoon turmeric powder

Salt to taste

2 tablespoons oil

2 star anise

2 bay leaves

10-12 curry leaves

Masala

2 tablespoons oil

1 cup grated coconut

25 shallots, peeled

1 inch ginger, chopped

12 garlic cloves, chopped

10 green chillies, chopped

2 dried red chillies, broken into bits

2 tablespoons coriander seeds

1 Clean and cut the chicken into medium-sized pieces (approximately twenty to twenty-four pieces). Rub in the turmeric powder and a little salt.

2 Heat two tablespoons of oil and fry the ingredients for the *masala* till light brown. Cool and grind to a smooth paste with a little water.

3 Heat the oil in a deep pan; add the star anise and bay leaves and sauté for half a minute.

4 Add the curry leaves and the marinated chicken. Sauté over high heat to seal the juices of the chicken.

5 Add the *masala* paste and mix thoroughly. Add one and a half cups of water and simmer till the chicken is almost cooked.

6 Add salt to taste, stir well and simmer till the chicken is tender and the gravy thickens.

Chef's Tip: Instead of using grated coconut, try making the dish with just coconut milk – the curry will be smoother and have a richer flavour.

fish in banana leaves

4 (100 grams each) pomfret fillets

Salt to taste

4 tablespoons lemon juice

1 cup chopped fresh coriander

4 green chillies, roughly chopped

¼ cup grated coconut

1 small onion, chopped

3 teaspoons cumin seeds

6-8 garlic cloves

3-4 banana leaves

1 Cut the fish fillets into two-inch by one-and-a-half inch pieces.

2 Sprinkle the salt and half the lemon juice and set aside for half an hour.

3 Grind the fresh coriander, green chillies, coconut, onion, cumin seeds and garlic to a fine paste. Add the salt and remaining lemon juice. Mix well.

4 Apply the ground paste to the fish fillets and marinate for at least fifteen minutes.

5 Cut the banana leaves into four pieces each.

6 Place one marinated fish piece on each piece of banana leaf along with a little of the ground paste and fold it.

7 Steam the fish in a steamer for fifteen minutes and serve hot.

iggaru royya

36 (350 grams) medium prawns

5 tablespoons oil

1 cup grated coconut

8 dried red chillies, broken into bits

1 teaspoon cumin seeds

½ teaspoon fenugreek seeds

10-12 black peppercorns

2 medium onions, chopped

2 teaspoons ginger paste

2 teaspoons garlic paste

2 medium tomatoes, chopped

Salt to taste

10-12 curry leaves

2 tablespoons chopped fresh coriander

1 Wash, peel and devein the prawns and pat them dry.

2 Heat two tablespoons of oil in a *kadai* and sauté the coconut, red chillies, cumin seeds, fenugreek seeds and peppercorns till the coconut turns light brown. Cool and grind to a coarse paste.

3 Heat the remaining oil in the same *kadai*; add the onions and sauté till golden brown. Add the ginger paste and garlic paste, and sauté till all the moisture evaporates. Add the ground paste and stir well.

4 Add the tomatoes, salt and curry leaves, and sauté over low heat for three to four minutes.

5 Add the prawns; mix well and cook till the prawns are tender. Garnish with the fresh coriander and serve hot.

Chef's Tip: Traditionally, this is a thick curry; but if you want to serve it with rice, thin the curry down with a little water.

malabar chemeen kari

25-30 small prawns, shelled, and deveined

1 teaspoon turmeric powder

Salt to taste

2 cups grated coconut

6 tablespoons oil

9-10 shallots, chopped

1 tablespoon red chilli powder

1 tablespoon coriander powder

6 green chillies, slit

4-6 curd chillies, slit

2 sprigs curry leaves

6 pieces *kodumpulli* (fish tamarind)

1 teaspoon fenugreek seeds, lightly pounded

4 whole dried red chillies

2 drumsticks, cut into 1-inch pieces

1 medium unripe mango, cut into wedges

1 Marinate the prawns in half a teaspoon of turmeric powder and little salt. Soak and grind the coconut with one cup of warm water and extract the thick milk and set aside. Reserve the coconut residue.

2 Heat four tablespoons of oil in a deep pan, add the onions and fry till transluscent. Add the chilli powder, remaining turmeric powder, coriander powder and stir. Add the green chillies, curd chillies, curry leaves and *kodumpulli*. Add the coconut residue and four cups of water. Boil till the gravy reduces by half and thickens. Set aside.

3 Heat the remaining oil in another pan, add pounded fenugreeks seeds and whole red chillies, and stir well. Add the marinated prawns, drumsticks and mango. Cook for two to three minutes or till the prawns are three-fourth done. Pour in the curry and cook for a few minutes. Add salt to taste.

4 Remove from heat and add the coconut milk and let it simmer for five minutes. Serve hot.

Note: To make the curd chillies, soak the chillies in a mixture of thin yogurt and salt for 6-8 hours. Dry in the sun till all the moisture dries up. Store in airtight tins. The chillies can be deep-fried and served as an accompaniment.

nalli nihari

500 grams lamb marrow bones

2½ tablespoons *Nihari Masala* (page 127)

1½ tablespoons rice bran oil

2 medium onions, sliced

1 tablespoon pure ghee

½ inch ginger, cut into thin strips

2 tablespoons wholewheat flour

Salt to taste

1 tablespoon lemon juice

2 tablespoons chopped fresh coriander

1 Heat the oil in a non-stick pan and sauté the onions till golden. Drain on absorbent paper.

2 Heat the ghee in a non-stick pressure cooker. Add the marrow bones and *nihari masala* and sauté for two minutes. Add four cups of water, close the lid and cook till pressure is released eight times (eight whistles). This may take about half an hour.

3 Remove the lid when the pressure has completely reduced and transfer the contents into a *kadai*. Bring the mixture to a boil. Add half the sautéed onions, and half the ginger and simmer for two minutes.

4 Combine the wholewheat flour with six tablespoons of water and mix well till smooth. Add to the marrow mixture and continue to simmer till the gravy thickens.

5 Add the salt and stir in the lemon juice.

6 Serve, garnished with the remaining sautéed onions, remaining ginger and fresh coriander.

dhania adrak champe

500 grams lamb chops

Marinade

½ small bunch (25 grams) fresh coriander

2 inches ginger

2 tablespoons chopped unripe papaya

½ teaspoon soda bicarbonate

10 fresh spinach leaves

4 green chillies

½ cup drained hung yogurt

1 tablespoon vinegar

1½ inches ginger, finely grated

5-6 black peppercorns, crushed

2 tablespoons roasted gram flour

Salt to taste

1 tablespoon oil

4 tablespoons melted butter

To Serve

Mint Chutney (page 126)

1 Pat the lamb chops dry with a kitchen towel. Flatten them with a rolling pin or with the back of a knife. Prick all over with a fork.

2 Grind the fresh coriander, ginger, papaya, soda bicarbonate, spinach and green chillies to a fine paste.

3 Place the ground paste in a bowl; add the yogurt, vinegar, grated ginger, crushed peppercorns, roasted gram flour, salt and oil, and mix well. Add the mutton chops; mix and set aside in a refrigerator to marinate overnight.

4 Preheat the oven to 180°C/350°F/Gas Mark 4 or heat a gas *tandoor* over a medium heat.

5 Place the marinated chops on a greased wire rack or grill and rub them with the marinade remaining in the bowl.

6 Grill the chops for twenty minutes, turning once in between. Baste with butter and grill for another fifteen minutes or till tender.

7 Serve with mint chutney.

spaghetti with chicken and pesto

200 grams spaghetti, boiled and drained

2 (200 grams each) chicken breasts, cut into 1-inch pieces

1 cup fresh basil

5-6 garlic cloves

¼ cup pine nuts

Salt to taste

4 tablespoons olive oil

⅓ cup Parmesan cheese shavings

3 tablespoons White Sauce (page 127)

¼ cup milk

1 To make the pesto sauce, process the basil, garlic, pine nuts, salt and two tablespoons of olive oil in a blender till smooth. Add the Parmesan cheese and process again.

2 Thin the white sauce with the milk and transfer to a pan and set aside.

3 Heat half a tablespoon of olive oil in a pan; add the spaghetti and toss to coat with the oil. Sprinkle a little salt and toss till heated through. Spread the spaghetti on a serving plate.

4 Heat the remaining olive oil; add the chicken and sauté for two to three minutes. Add the pesto and sauté over high heat. Add the white sauce and mix well. Season with salt and mix again. Cook for a few minutes till the chicken is tender.

5 Pour the sauce over the spaghetti and serve immediately.

rice & breads

tiranga kofta pulao

1½ cups Basmati rice, soaked

3 tablespoons ghee

3 small onions, sliced

Salt to taste

Paneer Kofta

150 grams cottage cheese, grated

Salt to taste

¼ teaspoon white pepper powder

½ teaspoon green cardamom powder

1½ tablespoons cornflour

Oil for deep-frying

Green Rice

1 medium bunch (200 grams) spinach

1 green chilli

2 garlic cloves

Salt to taste

White Rice

1 teaspoon cumin seeds

Yellow Rice

A few saffron threads

1 Mix the cottage cheese with the salt, pepper powder and cardamom powder and mash well. Divide into eighteen equal portions and shape into balls. Dust with cornflour.

2 Heat the oil in a *kadai* and deep-fry the cottage cheese balls till golden. Drain on absorbent paper.

3 Boil the rice with four cups of water till almost done; drain. Divide into three equal parts.

4 For the green rice, blanch spinach in plenty of water. Drain and purée in a blender along with the green chilli and garlic.

5 Heat one tablespoon of ghee in a pan; add one-third of the onions and sauté till translucent. Add the spinach purée and sauté for one minute over high heat. Add one part of the rice along with six cottage cheese balls and salt and toss to mix. Transfer to a bowl and set aside.

6 For the white rice, heat one tablespoon of ghee in a pan; add the cumin seeds and when they begin to change colour, add half the remaining onions and sauté till translucent. Add another part of rice, six cottage cheese balls and salt and toss well. Transfer to a separate bowl and set aside.

7 For the yellow rice, soak the saffron in two tablespoons of water. Heat one tablespoon of ghee in a pan; add the remaining onions and sauté till translucent. Add the remaining rice with the saffron water. Add the remaining cottage cheese balls and salt and toss to mix. Transfer to a bowl and set aside.

8 In a transparent square glass dish, spread a layer of green rice and level the surface. Spread a layer of white rice over the green rice and level the surface. Top with a layer of yellow rice. Alternatively, arrange the rice in a pattern on a flat dish.

coconut rice

1 cup grated coconut

1½ cups rice, soaked

1 tablespoon ghee

6-8 cashew nuts

4 tablespoons oil

½ teaspoon mustard seeds

1 teaspoon skinless split black gram

2 dried red chillies, broken into two

10-12 curry leaves

1 medium onion, finely chopped

2 green chillies, finely chopped

1 inch ginger, finely chopped

Salt to taste

2 tablespoons chopped fresh coriander

1 teaspoon coconut oil (optional)

1 Boil sufficient water in a deep pan and cook the rice, stirring frequently, till almost done. Drain and spread out on a flat plate to cool.

2 Heat the ghee in a small pan and stir-fry the cashew nuts till light brown and set aside.

3 Heat the oil in a *kadai* and add the mustard seeds. When they begin to splutter, add the split black gram, red chillies and curry leaves and sauté for a few seconds.

4 Add the onion, green chillies and ginger, and sauté for two to three minutes, or until the onion is translucent. Add the coconut and cook over medium heat for two minutes. Add the cooked rice, salt and chopped coriander and toss well to mix. Cook till the rice is heated through.

5 Drizzle with the coconut oil and mix lightly. Serve hot, garnished with the fried cashew nuts.

shahi prawn pulao

300 grams medium prawns, peeled and deveined

1½ cups Basmati rice, soaked

4 tablespoons oil

3 large onions, sliced

2 teaspoons ginger-garlic paste

2 medium tomatoes, chopped

2 green chillies, slit

2 teaspoons red chilli powder

½ teaspoon turmeric powder

Salt to taste

½ cup Coconut Milk (page 127)

¼ cup yogurt

1 teaspoon *garam masala* powder

1 tablespoon chopped fresh coriander

1 Heat the oil in a pressure cooker. Add the onions and sauté till pale gold. Add the ginger-garlic paste and sauté for one minute.

2 Add the tomatoes and continue to sauté till the tomatoes soften.

3 Add the green chillies and chilli powder and sauté till the oil begins to separate.

4 Add the turmeric powder, prawns and salt. Sauté for two minutes and stir in the coconut milk and yogurt. Add the *garam masala* powder, stir and simmer for two minutes over low heat.

5 Add the drained rice and stir lightly. Add two cups of water and bring to a boil. Seal the cooker with the lid and cook over medium heat till the pressure is released twice (two whistles).

6 Remove the lid when the pressure has reduced completely, garnish with fresh coriander and serve hot.

chanar pulao

400 grams cottage cheese, cut into 1-inch cubes

1½ cups Basmati rice

3 tablespoons ghee

2 teaspoons sugar

1 large onion, finely sliced

1 bay leaf

1 inch cinnamon

2 cloves

2 green cardamoms

Salt to taste

1 Wash and drain the rice and spread out to dry. When completely dry, add one tablespoon of ghee and the sugar and mix well.

2 Heat one tablespoon of ghee in a pan and sauté the cottage cheese cubes. Drain and set aside.

3 Add the remaining ghee to the same pan and sauté the onion till crisp and brown. Drain and set aside.

4 To the ghee remaining in the pan, add the bay leaf, cinnamon, cloves and cardamoms and sauté till fragrant. Add the rice and salt and sauté for two or three minutes.

5 Add three cups of hot water and bring to a boil. Lower heat, cover and cook till the rice is done and all the water has been absorbed.

6 Add the cottage cheese cubes and stir lightly to mix. Sprinkle fried onions and serve.

Chanar Pulao

kachche gosht ki biryani

1 kilogram mutton or lamb on the bone, cut into 2-inch pieces

2 cups Basmati rice, soaked

2 two-inch pieces ginger

20-25 garlic cloves

½ cup fresh mint

A few saffron threads

3 tablespoons milk

2 cups yogurt

2 green chillies, chopped

2 teaspoons red chilli powder

1 teaspoon turmeric powder

Salt to taste

4-5 large onions, sliced and deep-fried till golden brown

5-6 cloves

1 inch cinnamon

5 green cardamoms

1 black cardamom

10 black peppercorns

¼ cup *Potli Masala* (page 127)

½ teaspoon caraway seeds

½ teaspoon green cardamom powder

2 teaspoons *garam masala* powder

½ cup chopped fresh coriander

5 tablespoons pure ghee

2 tablespoons rose petals

1 teaspoon rose water

1 teaspoon screw pine essence

Wholewheat flour dough to seal the pan

1 Grind half the ginger and garlic to a fine paste. Cut the remaining ginger into fine strips. Chop half the fresh mint. Warm the milk slightly and soak the saffron in it.

2 In a bowl, mix together the mutton, yogurt, ginger-garlic paste, green chillies, chilli powder, turmeric powder, salt, one-third of the fried sliced onions and the chopped fresh mint. Leave to marinate for one hour.

3 Bring five cups of water to a boil in a separate pan. Place the cloves, cinnamon, green and black cardamoms, peppercorns and *potli masala* in a piece of muslin and tie up in a *potli*. Add the *potli* to the boiling water. Add salt to taste, the caraway seeds and soaked rice. Bring to a boil and cook till partially done. Drain.

4 Arrange half the marinated mutton in a thick-bottomed pan. Spread half the rice over the mutton. Top with one-third of the fried sliced onions and ginger strips. Sprinkle half the green cardamom powder, *garam masala* powder and chopped coriander on top. Roughly tear half the remaining fresh mint and sprinkle over the rice. Pour half the ghee over everything.

5 Add half the saffron-flavoured milk to the pan. Sprinkle with half the rose petals, rose water and screw pine essence. Repeat the layers once again. Cover the pan and seal the lid with wholewheat flour dough. Cook over high heat for five minutes, then lower the heat. Place the pan on a *tawa* and cook over low heat for forty-five minutes. Serve hot with *raita*.

kachche murgh ki biryani

800 grams boneless chicken, cut into 1½-inch pieces
1½ cups Basmati rice, soaked
Oil for deep-frying
4-5 large onions, sliced
1½ cups yogurt
Salt to taste
1 tablespoon garlic paste
1 tablespoon ginger paste
2 green chillies, chopped
½ teaspoon turmeric powder
1 teaspoon red chilli powder
2 teaspoons *garam masala* powder
½ cup fresh mint leaves, roughly torn
½ teaspoon caraway seeds
10 cloves
10 green cardamoms
5 black cardamoms
2 one-inch sticks cinnamon
2 inches ginger, cut into thin strips
A few saffron threads
3 tablespoons milk
½ cup chopped fresh coriander
2 tablespoon dried rose petals
1 teaspoon screw pine water
1 teaspoon rose water
½ teaspoon green cardamom powder

1 Soak the *matka* (earthenware pot) in water for two to three hours. Remove and place upside down to dry.

2 Heat the oil in a *kadai* and deep fry the onions till golden. Drain on absorbent paper.

3 In a bowl, mix together the chicken, yogurt, salt, garlic paste, ginger paste, green chillies, turmeric powder, chilli powder, half the *garam masala* powder, half the mint leaves and half the fried onions. Leave to marinate for about an hour.

4 Heat four cups of water in a pan; add the salt and caraway seeds. Tie the cloves, green and black cardamoms and cinnamon in a piece of muslin and pound lightly. Add the *potli* to the water in the pan and bring to a boil. Add the rice and cook till three-fourth done. Drain.

5 Preheat an oven to 200°C/400°F/Gas Mark 6.

6 Place half the chicken in the *matka*. Spread a layer of half the rice over the chicken. Sprinkle half the ginger strips, saffron-flavoured milk, fresh coriander, remaining mint leaves, dried rose petals, screw pine essence, rose water, cardamom powder and fried onions. Spread the remaining chicken over the rice. Spread the remaining rice over the chicken and sprinkle the remaining ginger strips, saffron-flavoured milk, coriander leaves, mint leaves, dried rose petals, screw pine essence, rose water, cardamom powder and fried onions.

7 Place the *matka* on heat and cook till bubbling. Cover tightly and seal the lid with some *atta* dough. Place in the oven and cook for twenty to twenty-five minutes.

8 Turn the heat off in the oven and leave the pot in the oven till ready to serve. Serve the *biryani* directly from the *matka*.

spicy chicken fried rice on crispy basil leaves

200 grams minced chicken

2½ cups cooked rice

½ cup fresh basil

2 fresh red chillies

4 green chillies

7-8 garlic cloves

3 tablespoons oil

1 teaspoon fish sauce

1 teaspoon sugar

1 hard-boiled egg, sliced vertically

1 Pound one red and two green chillies and the garlic with a mortar and pestle. Cut the remaining red chilli and green chillies into thin diagonal slices.

2 Heat the oil in a wok; add the basil and fry till crisp. Drain and set aside.

3 Add the chilli-garlic mixture to the same oil and sauté until fragrant. Add the minced chicken and stir-fry for three to four minutes.

4 Add the fish sauce and sugar and continue to stir-fry for a minute. Add the rice and continue to stir-fry.

5 When the rice is heated through, add the red and green chilli slices and mix thoroughly.

6 Place the fried basil on a plate, spread the rice over the leaves and serve, garnished with the egg slices.

spinach and mushroom risotto

1½ cups parboiled rice

½ bunch (125 grams) spinach, roughly chopped

4-5 fresh button mushrooms, sliced

5 tablespoons butter

1 medium onion, chopped

4-5 garlic cloves, chopped

1 cup white wine

3½ cups Vegetable Stock (page 126) or water

Salt to taste

¾ cup grated Parmesan cheese

½ teaspoon pepper powder

½ cup fresh cream

1 Wash and soak the rice for two hours. Drain.

2 Mix together three tablespoons of butter, the onion, garlic and mushrooms in a deep microwave-safe dish. Cook, uncovered, on HIGH (100%) for three minutes.

3 Add the rice, wine, half the stock and salt and cook on HIGH (100%) for ten minutes.

4 Stir in the remaining stock and cook on HIGH (100%) for another ten minutes.

5 Stir in the spinach, cheese, pepper powder and cream and mix well. Cook, uncovered, on HIGH (100%) for two minutes.

6 Mix in the remaining two tablespoons of butter and serve hot.

Chef's Tip: This is a speedy version of the original recipe. Traditionally risotto is made with arborio rice and cooked over a low heat adding the stock a little by little.

chole biryani

1½ cups Basmati rice
1 cup chickpeas
2 tablespoons tea leaves
Salt to taste
5-6 green cardamoms
2-3 bay leaves
2-3 cloves
1½ cups yogurt
1 teaspoon ginger paste
1 inch ginger, cut into thin strips
½ cup fresh mint, roughly torn
1 teaspoon green chilli paste
1 teaspoon red chilli powder
1 teaspoon turmeric powder
1 teaspoon *garam masala* powder
1 teaspoon garlic paste
A few saffron threads
1 tablespoon warm milk
A few drops of screw pine essence
¼ cup chopped fresh coriander

1 Soak the chickpeas overnight in four cups of water. Drain and pressure cook in four cups of water with salt and the tea leaves tied in a piece of muslin *(potli)*, till tender. Remove the muslin bag *(potli)* and drain the chickpeas.

2 Soak the rice in three cups of water for about half an hour. Drain. Boil four cups of water in a deep pan with the salt and green cardamoms, bay leaves and cloves. Add the rice and cook till half done. Drain excess water.

3 Marinate the boiled chickpeas in the mixture of yogurt, ginger paste, ginger strips, half the fresh mint, green chilli paste, chilli powder, turmeric powder, *garam masala* powder and garlic paste.

4 Dissolve the saffron in warm milk and mix with the screw pine essence.

5 Place the marinated chickpeas in a deep non-stick pan.

6 Spread the half-cooked rice over the chickpeas evenly. Sprinkle the saffron-screw pine mixture and half the chopped coriander over the rice.

7 Cover the pan tightly and cook on low heat for fifteen minutes or till the rice is cooked.

8 Serve hot, garnished with the remaining fresh coriander and mint leaves.

paneer aur pudina naan

4 cups refined flour

1 teaspoon baking powder

½ teaspoon soda bicarbonate

Salt to taste

2 teaspoons sugar

1 egg

1 cup milk

2 tablespoons yogurt

2 tablespoons oil

2 teaspoons onion seeds

Butter, to serve

Stuffing

800 grams cottage cheese, grated

½ cup Mint Chutney (page 126)

3 tablespoons oil

2 teaspoons cumin seeds

2 medium onions, chopped

4 green chillies, chopped

Salt to taste

1 Sift the refined flour with the baking powder, soda bicarbonate and salt into a deep bowl. Add the sugar, egg, milk, yogurt and a little water and knead into a medium soft dough.

2 Brush with the oil, cover with a damp piece of muslin and set aside for one hour.

3 For the stuffing, heat the oil in a pan. Add the cumin seeds and when they begin to change colour, add the onions and green chillies and sauté over medium heat for one minute.

4 Add the mint chutney and continue to sauté for another minute. Add the grated cottage cheese and salt, toss well and transfer to a plate to cool. Divide into eight equal portions.

5 Knead the dough again and divide it into eight equal portions. Shape into round balls and dust with flour. Flatten each ball and roll out into four-inch rounds.

6 Place one portion of the stuffing in the centre, gather the edges together and shape into a ball again. Sprinkle one-fourth teaspoon of onion seeds, press lightly and roll out into a seven-inch round.

7 Heat a pressure cooker. Moisten one side of the *naan* with wet fingers and gently stick the moistened side to the inner wall of the pressure cooker. Make sure the *naan* is moist enough to stick.

8 Place the cooker upside down over an open flame to make a kind of *tandoor*. Cook over high heat for two to three minutes, lower heat and cook for two to three minutes more.

9 Turn the cooker upright and gently dislodge the *naan* from the cooker wall. Cut into quarters and serve hot with a dollop of butter.

chicken missi roti

1½ cups minced chicken

1 cup wholewheat flour

1 cup gram flour

Salt to taste

1 teaspoon turmeric powder

1 teaspoon *chaat masala*

4 green chillies, chopped

1 tablespoon dried pomegranate seeds

1 medium onion, finely chopped

2 tablespoons chopped fresh coriander

1 egg

1 tablespoon oil + for shallow-frying

1 Mix the wholewheat flour, gram flour, salt, turmeric powder, *chaat masala*, green chillies, dried pomegranate seeds, onion, fresh coriander, minced chicken and egg. Add a little oil and just enough water to knead into a soft dough.

2 Divide the dough into equal portions. Grease your palms and roll the portions into balls.

3 Heat a *tawa*. Roll each ball in some flour and roll out into a thick *roti*. Place on the hot *tawa* and cook over medium heat on both sides.

4 Drizzle some oil around the *roti* and when one side turns golden brown, flip it over and drizzle some more oil, cooking the other side till golden brown. Serve immediately.

5 Alternatively, apply a little oil to the dough balls and grease the worktop. With greased fingers, gently pat each ball of dough into a slightly thick *roti* and cook on the *tawa* as above.

dal & kadhi

palak ki kadhi

½ medium bunch (100 grams) spinach, chopped

2 cups yogurt, whisked

4 tablespoons gram flour

2 tablespoons oil

1 teaspoon cumin seeds

½ teaspoon fenugreek seeds

A pinch of asafoetida

1 large onion, chopped

1 teaspoon ginger paste

3 green chillies, chopped

¼ teaspoon turmeric powder

½ teaspoon red chilli powder

Salt to taste

1 teaspoon sugar (optional)

1 Whisk together the yogurt, gram flour and three cups of water till smooth.

2 Heat the oil in a non-stick pan and add the cumin seeds and fenugreek seeds. When the seeds begin to change colour, add the asafoetida and onion and sauté for two minutes.

3 Add the ginger paste and green chillies and sauté for half a minute. Add the turmeric powder, chilli powder and spinach and sauté for two minutes.

4 Add the yogurt mixture and bring to a boil. Add the salt and sugar, lower the heat and simmer for ten to fifteen minutes, or till the *kadhi* thickens. Serve hot.

rajasthani panchmel dal

¼ cup split Bengal gram

¼ cup whole green gram

¼ cup split black gram

¼ cup split pigeon peas

¼ cup whole red lentils

Salt to taste

½ teaspoon turmeric powder

3 tablespoons oil

A pinch of asafoetida

½ teaspoon cumin seeds

4-5 cloves

2 dried red chillies, broken into large bits

1 teaspoon green chilli-ginger paste

1 teaspoon roasted cumin powder

1 teaspoon coriander powder

½ teaspoon red chilli powder

2 medium tomatoes, chopped

½ teaspoon *garam masala* powder

2 tablespoons chopped fresh coriander

1 Soak the pulses in three cups of water for at least two hours. Drain and boil in three cups of water with salt and the turmeric powder till tender.

2 Heat the oil in a pan; add the asafoetida, cumin seeds, cloves and red chillies. When the cumin seeds begin to change colour, add the green chilli-ginger paste and sauté for one minute.

3 Add the cumin powder, coriander powder and chilli powder and mix well. Add the tomatoes and cook till the oil separates. Stir in the cooked pulses, salt and more water, if required. Cook for ten minutes, stirring occasionally.

4 Add the *garam masala* powder and serve hot, garnished with chopped coriander.

char dal ka dalcha

¼ cup split Bengal gram

2 tablespoons split lentils

¼ cup split pigeon peas

2 tablespoons split green gram

1 teaspoon turmeric powder

1½ teaspoons red chilli powder

Salt to taste

1 lemon-sized ball tamarind

3 tablespoons oil

2 medium onions, sliced

2 teaspoons ginger paste

5-6 green chillies, slit

400 grams bottle gourd, cut into 1-inch pieces

Seasoning

2 tablespoons ghee

1 teaspoon cumin seeds

5-6 dried red chillies, broken in half

12-15 curry leaves

6-8 garlic cloves, chopped

1 Soak all the pulses in plenty of water for at least half an hour. Drain and place in a pressure cooker with half a teaspoon of turmeric powder, half a teaspoon of chilli powder, salt and four cups of water. Pressure-cook for four or five minutes, or till completely cooked.

2 Soak the tamarind in one cup of warm water for half an hour. Squeeze out the pulp, strain and set aside.

3 Heat the oil in a pan; add the onions and sauté till light brown. Add the remaining chilli and turmeric powders, the ginger paste and slit green chillies. Sauté for a few seconds and add the bottle gourd.

4 Sauté for three or four minutes and add the cooked pulses. Cook, covered, over medium heat for about ten minutes, or till the bottle gourd is tender. Add the tamarind pulp and half a cup of water and cook over medium heat for four or five minutes, stirring occasionally. Lower the heat and simmer for another five minutes.

5 For the seasoning, heat the ghee in a small pan; add the cumin seeds and when they begin to change colour, add the red chillies and curry leaves. Sauté for a few seconds; add the garlic and sauté till the garlic turns light brown.

6 Pour the mixture into the *dal*, cover the pan with a lid immediately to trap the flavours. Serve hot.

aamras ki kadhi

1 cup unripe mango pulp

1 cup ripe mango pulp

3 tablespoons gram flour

Salt to taste

1 cup buttermilk

1 tablespoon oil

A pinch of asafoetida

½ teaspoon mustard seeds

¼ teaspoon fenugreek seeds

6-8 curry leaves

2 green chillies, slit

½ cup *boondi*

1 Mix together the unripe and ripe mango pulp, the gram flour and salt till smooth. Stir in the buttermilk.

2 Heat the oil in a deep pan; add the asafoetida, mustard seeds and fenugreek seeds and sauté till the mustard seeds begin to splutter. Add the curry leaves and green chillies and sauté for two minutes.

3 Stir in the mango mixture. Add a little water if required and bring to a boil. Lower the heat and simmer for ten to fifteen minutes. Add approximately two cups of water to get the desired consistency.

4 Add the *boondi* and simmer for five more minutes. Serve hot.

dal lucknowi

1 cup split pigeon peas, soaked

2 green chillies, chopped

½ teaspoon turmeric powder

Salt to taste

2 tablespoons oil

1 teaspoon cumin seeds

4 dried red chillies, broken into large bits

5 garlic cloves, chopped

A pinch of asafoetida

1 cup milk

2 tablespoons chopped fresh coriander

1 Pressure-cook the pigeon peas and green chillies with two cups of water till the pressure is released twice (two whistles).

2 Remove the lid when the pressure has completely reduced. Add the turmeric powder and salt and bring to a boil; lower heat and continue to cook.

3 Heat the oil in a small pan; add the cumin seeds, red chillies, garlic and asafoetida and sauté till fragrant.

4 Pour the sizzling spices into the simmering *dal* and mix well. Stir in the milk and one cup of water and continue to simmer for two or three minutes.

5 Adjust salt, garnish with fresh coriander and serve hot.

mutton dhansaak

450 grams boneless lean lamb or mutton, cubed

¼ cup split pigeon peas

¼ cup split red lentils

2 medium onions, sliced

1 inch ginger, chopped

5–6 garlic cloves, chopped

10 black peppercorns

2 green chillies, slit and seeded

½ teaspoon turmeric powder

1 teaspoon red chilli powder

100 grams pumpkin, cut into ½-inch cubes

3 medium brinjals, cut into ½-inch cubes

1 large potato, cut into ½-inch cubes

1 teaspoon salt

¼ medium bunch (60 grams) fenugreek leaves, chopped

10-15 fresh mint leaves, chopped

2 medium tomatoes, chopped

2 tablespoons *dhansaak masala*

3 tablespoons Tamarind Pulp (page 126)

2 tablespoons chopped fresh coriander

1 Soak the pulses in two cups of water for thirty minutes. Drain.

2 Heat a non-stick pan; add the onions and roast on low heat for two to three minutes. Add the ginger and garlic and stir for three to four minutes.

3 Add the lamb cubes and continue to cook for eight to ten minutes, until the meat is lightly browned on all sides.

4 Stir in the peppercorns, chillies, turmeric powder and chilli powder. Add the soaked pulses and mix well.

5 Add the pumpkin, brinjals, potato, salt and three and a half cups of water; bring to a boil and cook for ten minutes.

6 Stir in the fenugreek and mint leaves, followed by the tomatoes. Cover and cook over low heat until the mutton is cooked – this may take thirty to forty five minutes. If you are using a pressure cooker, cook till pressure is released six times (six whistles).

7 Once the lamb is cooked, switch off the heat and remove the meat from the mixture. Stir in the *dhansaak masala* and tamarind pulp.

8 Pour the mixture from the pan into a blender and blend until smooth. Transfer back into the pan and add the lamb. If necessary, adjust the consistency by adding water. Sprinkle the chopped coriander and cook for another five minutes.

9 Serve hot with brown rice.

dal hari-bhari

1 cup split green gram

1 medium bunch (200 grams) fresh spinach leaves, chopped

1 medium bunch (250 grams) fresh fenugreek leaves, chopped

3 tablespoons chopped fresh coriander

½ teaspoon turmeric powder

Salt to taste

6 garlic cloves, chopped

3 green chillies, chopped

1 inch ginger, chopped

2 tablespoons pure ghee

1 teaspoon cumin seeds

2 medium onions, chopped

2 medium tomatoes, chopped

¾ teaspoon red chilli powder

1 tablespoon lemon juice

1 Soak the *dal* in two cups of water for one hour. Pressure-cook with the turmeric powder and salt till the pressure is released twice (two whistles). Remove the lid when the pressure has completely reduced and mash the *dal* with the back of a ladle.

2 Grind the garlic, green chillies and ginger to a paste.

3 Heat the ghee in a pan and add the cumin seeds. When the seeds begin to change colour, add the onions and sauté till light brown. Add the tomatoes, chilli powder and ground paste. Sauté till tomatoes soften.

4 Add the fresh spinach, fenugreek and coriander and sauté for four or five minutes.

5 Stir in the cooked *dal* and one cup of water and bring the mixture to a boil. Stir in the lemon juice.

6 Cook for four or five minutes, stirring continuously. Serve hot with rice.

quick sindhi kadhi

¾ cup gram flour

5 tablespoons oil

1 teaspoon cumin seeds

1½ teaspoons red chilli powder

½ teaspoon turmeric powder

½ teaspoon fenugreek seeds

4-5 green chillies, slit

¼ teaspoon asafoetida, optional

4 medium tomatoes, halved

100 grams cluster beans

8-10 ladies' fingers, slit

8-10 curry leaves

Salt to taste

2 tablespoons Tamarind Pulp (page 126)

2 tablespoons chopped fresh coriander

1 Mix the gram flour and one and a half cups of water till smooth.

2 Put the oil, cumin seeds, chilli powder, turmeric powder, fenugreek seeds, green chillies and asafoetida into a microwave-safe bowl. Cook, uncovered, on HIGH (100%) for two minutes.

3 Add the tomatoes, cluster beans, ladies' fingers, curry leaves, gram flour mixture and salt and mix well. Cook, uncovered, on HIGH (100%) for three minutes.

4 Stir in one cup of water, the tamarind pulp and fresh coriander and cook on HIGH (100%) for two minutes.

5 Serve hot with steamed rice.

maa chole di dal

½ cup split black gram

½ cup split Bengal gram

Salt to taste

¼ teaspoon turmeric powder

1 inch ginger, chopped

3 green chillies, chopped

2-3 tablespoons pure ghee

1 tablespoon butter

1 teaspoon cumin seeds

1 medium onion, chopped

2 medium tomatoes, chopped

½ teaspoon red chilli powder

2 tablespoons chopped fresh coriander

1 Mix the two lentils, wash and soak in four cups of water for one hour. Drain.

2 Place the soaked lentils, in a pan with four cups of water, salt to taste, turmeric powder, half the ginger and half the green chillies. Cover and cook over a low heat till the lentils are tender. Stir well with a ladle to mix well without mashing the *dal*.

3 Heat the ghee and butter in a pan; add the cumin seeds, remaining green chillies and ginger. Stir and add the onion and sauté till light brown.

4 Add the tomatoes and sauté till they soften. Add the chilli powder and sauté for half a minute.

5 Add the sizzling seasoning to the *dal* and mix well. Simmer for a few minutes and serve hot, garnished with the coriander.

pickles & chutneys

sarson ki chutney

½ cup mustard seeds

1½ cups + 4 tablespoons vinegar

Salt to taste

1 tablespoon sugar

¼ teaspoon turmeric powder

1 Grind the mustard seeds with four tablespoons of vinegar to a fine paste.

2 Pour the remaining vinegar into a pan. Add the salt, sugar and turmeric powder and bring to a boil.

3 Add the mustard paste and cook for fifteen to twenty minutes or till thick.

4 Cool and serve.

Chef's Tip: For best results, leave the chutney for two days to allow the flavours to develop and mature.

keri ki launjee

1 kg unripe mangoes

3 tablespoons mustard oil

¾ teaspoon fenugreek seeds

4 teaspoons fennel seeds

½ teaspoon onion seeds

1 teaspoon coriander powder

1 teaspoon red chilli powder

½ teaspoon turmeric powder

Salt to taste

1¼ cups grated jaggery

1 Peel the mangoes, cut lengthways into quarters and remove the seeds.

2 Heat the oil in a *kadai* to smoking point. Lower the heat to medium, add the fenugreek seeds and sauté till they begin to change colour.

3 Add the fennel seeds, onion seeds, coriander powder, chilli powder, turmeric powder and salt. Mix well.

4 Add the mangoes and sauté for five minutes. Add the jaggery and half a cup of water. Bring to a boil, cover the pan and simmer, stirring occasionally, for seven or eight minutes.

5 Remove and set aside to cool. Store in sterilised bottles when completely cold.

spinach chutney

1 medium bunch (250 grams) spinach, roughly chopped

1 teaspoon oil

1 tablespoon skinless split black gram

1 tablespoon split Bengal gram

4 dried red chillies

¼ teaspoon asafoetida

1 medium onion, chopped

1 medium tomato, chopped

1 green chilli, chopped

4 tablespoons grated coconut

1 teaspoon Tamarind Pulp (page 126)

Salt to taste

1 Heat the oil in a pan; add the split black gram and split Bengal gram and roast to a golden brown.

2 Add the red chillies, asafoetida, onion, tomato and green chilli; sauté for five minutes.

3 Add the spinach, coconut, tamarind pulp and salt and mix well.

4 Remove from heat and cool. Grind to a fine paste and serve.

burnt garlic and mint chutney

20-25 garlic cloves

3 cups fresh mint, roughly torn

1 tablespoon oil

½ teaspoon black salt

1 inch ginger, roughly chopped

2 green chillies, roughly chopped

1½ cups yogurt, whisked

1 tablespoon lemon juice

Salt to taste

1 Heat the oil in a pan; add the garlic and sauté. Sprinkle black salt and sauté till well browned.

2 Grind together the mint, ginger, green chillies, sautéed garlic and two tablespoons of water to a fine paste.

3 Add the paste to the yogurt and mix well. Add the lemon juice and salt and mix again.

4 Pass the mixture through a piece of muslin, squeezing well to get a smooth chutney.

5 Serve chilled.

lemon and date pickle

10 lemons

225 grams dates, stoned and roughly chopped

2 tablespoons vinegar

1½ tablespoons salt

3½ tablespoons sugar

4 garlic cloves

1 inch ginger, chopped

4 tablespoons oil

1 teaspoon cumin seeds

2 teaspoons mustard seeds

2 tablespoons red chilli powder

1 Wash, wipe dry, quarter the lemons and remove all the pips. Place them in a pan along with the vinegar, salt and sugar. Cover the pan and simmer over low heat until the lemons have softened. Remove the lemons and reserve the liquid.

2 Wipe the garlic and ginger dry and grind them along with the dates to a smooth paste.

3 Heat the oil in a pan and sauté the cumin seeds and mustard seeds. Remove from heat and add the reserved liquid used to cook the lemons.

4 Add the chilli powder and return to the heat and stir for a minute.

5 Slowly add the ground date-ginger-garlic paste and one-fourth cup of water and mix well. Finally add the lemons, bring to a boil and cook for a few minutes.

6 Remove from heat and set aside to cool. Pour into a heated sterilised jar and seal while warm.

desserts

tiramisù

12 slices (175 grams) chocolate sponge cake

½ tablespoon unflavoured gelatine

1 cup thick cream

½ cup powdered sugar

3 egg yolks

¼ cup sugar

2 tablespoons + 2 teaspoons instant coffee powder

¾ cup mascarpone cheese

Chocolate curls, to decorate

1 Cut each slice of cake in half.

2 Dissolve the gelatine in three tablespoons of hot water. Whip the cream with powdered sugar till stiff and set aside.

3 Whip the egg yolks with sugar and one tablespoon of water in a double-boiler or in a heatproof bowl over a pan of simmering water, till the mixture forms thick ribbons. Set aside to cool.

4 Mix two tablespoons of instant coffee powder in half a cup of water and soak the chocolate sponge fingers in the solution.

5 Arrange half the sponge fingers in a layer at the base of a springform tin.

6 Mix two teaspoons of instant coffee powder in one teaspoon of water. Add this along with the mascarpone cheese and dissolved gelatine to the egg mixture and mix well. Fold in the whipped cream.

7 Pour half the mixture over the chocolate fingers. Arrange the remaining chocolate fingers over, and top with the remaining coffee mixture, levelling the top.

8 Place in the refrigerator till set. Remove from the tin, cut into wedges and serve chilled, decorated with chocolate curls.

Chef's Tip

A springform tin is a round cake tin with a removable base. You can also set the dessert in individual moulds.

black forest gâteau

½ cup refined flour

2 tablespoons cocoa powder

3 eggs

6 tablespoons sugar

1 teaspoon baking powder

¼ cup milk

1 cup whipping cream

Chocolate curls

½ cup tinned cherries

1 Preheat the oven to 180°C/350°F/Gas Mark 4. Line and grease a deep eight-inch round cake tin.

2 Beat together the eggs and sugar for eight to ten minutes, or until thick and pale. Sift the flour and cocoa over the egg mixture and fold in gently, adding the milk as you mix.

3 Transfer the batter to the cake tin. Bake for thirty minutes, or until springy to the touch. Remove from the oven and leave the cake in the tin for five minutes to cool slightly. Turn out onto a wire rack; peel off the paper base and leave to cool.

4 Cut the cake in half horizontally and sprinkle each half with cherry syrup from the tinned cherries. Whip the cream until stiff.

5 Place the bottom half of the cake on a serving plate and spread half the whipped cream over it. Cover with the top half of the cake. Use the remaining cream to cover the top and sides.

6 Decorate the gâteau with chocolate curls and cherries and chill in the refrigerator.

eggless pineapple mousse

6 slices canned pineapple, at room temperature

2 teaspoons gelatine

½ tin (200 grams) sweetened condensed milk

3 teaspoons lemon juice

250 grams cream

A few drops pineapple essence

A few drops of edible yellow colour

1 tablespoon powdered sugar

Glacé cherries, as required

1 Mix the gelatine with half cup water in a small pan. Heat on low heat, stirring continuously, till it dissolves.

2 Pour the condensed milk in a bowl and beat till light and creamy. In another bowl, mix the lemon juice with half a cup of pineapple syrup from the tin.

3 Chop five slices of pineapple. Add the pineapple syrup and pineapple to the condensed milk.

4 Pour the gelatine solution into the condensed milk mixture stirring continuously. Freeze the mixture for half an hour till it is thick.

5 Remove from the freezer and beat till smooth. Add two hundred grams of cream and reserve the remaining cream for decoration.

6 Add the pineapple essence and yellow colour, beat well and put it back in the freezer for fifteen to twenty minutes.

7 Remove from the freezer and beat again till smooth. Pour into a serving dish and freeze for one hour or till set.

8 Whip the reserved cream with powdered sugar.

9 Remove the mousse from the freezer. Transfer the whipped cream in a piping bag fitted with a star nozzle and make rosettes on the surface of the mousse. Place a glacé cherry on each rosette and serve immediately.

coconut custard

1½ cups Coconut Milk (page 126)

4 eggs

5 tablespoons brown sugar

1 teaspoon vanilla essence

Icing sugar, to decorate

1 Preheat the oven to 150°C/300°F/Gas Mark 2.

2 Whisk the eggs and sugar in a bowl until fluffy.

3 Add the coconut milk and vanilla essence and continue to whisk till well blended.

4 Strain the mixture and pour into four individual ramekins (small individual moulds).

5 Pour some water into a baking tray, place the moulds in the tray and cover with greaseproof paper so that a crust does not form on top. Pierce the greaseproof paper at intervals to allow the steam to escape.

6 Place the tray in the oven and bake for forty to forty-five minutes. Remove from the oven and leave to cool in the moulds.

7 Turn out onto dessert plates, sprinkle generously with icing sugar and serve.

mysore paak

¾ cup gram flour

4 cups sugar

2½ cups pure ghee

1 Sift the gram flour twice. Heat the ghee in a pan and keep it hot over very low heat.

2 Cook the sugar with two and a half cups of water over medium heat, stirring continuously till it dissolves. Increase the heat and bring the syrup to a boil. Cook without stirring for about five minutes, or till it reaches a single-thread consistency.

3 Add half a cup of hot ghee to the syrup and stir; add the gram flour gradually, stirring all the while to prevent lumps from forming.

4 Stir continuously till the mixture starts bubbling.

5 Pour in the remaining hot ghee, half a cup at a time. Every time you add the ghee, the mixture should sizzle and froth.

6 Continue this process till all the ghee has been used up and there is a pleasant sweet roasted aroma.

7 Pour the mixture into a greased tray. Cool a little and cut into squares.

8 Separate the squares when completely cold and store in an airtight container to retain their freshness and crispness.

sitaphal basoondi

1½ litres milk

1 cup custard apple pulp

½ cup sugar

1 tablespoon cudpah nuts

½ teaspoon green cardamom powder

10-12 pistachios, sliced

10-12 almonds, blanched and slivered

3-4 rose petals (optional)

1 Bring the milk to a boil in a heavy-bottomed pan on high heat. Lower the heat and simmer for half an hour, stirring continuously, to prevent the milk from burning and sticking to the bottom of the pan.

2 When the milk reduces to half the original quantity, add the sugar. Simmer for five more minutes. Remove from heat and set aside to cool.

3 Add the custard apple, cardamom powder, sliced pistachios and cudpah nuts to the cooled milk.

4 Transfer to a serving bowl and garnish with almond slivers and rose petals. Serve cold.

zafrani sevian

6 tablespoons vermicelli

10-15 saffron threads

1½ litres milk

8 tablespoons sugar

20 raisins

1 teaspoon green cardamom powder

1 tablespoon toasted almond slivers

1 Heat a non-stick pan and roast the vermicelli on medium heat till lightly browned.

2 Bring the milk to a boil in a deep pan. Lower the heat and simmer for two to three minutes.

3 Add the sugar and cook till it dissolves. Add the vermicelli and raisins and cook for two minutes.

4 Take it off the heat. Add the saffron and cardamom powder and stir well.

5 Serve hot or cold, garnished with toasted almond slivers.

Zafrani Sevian

khubani ka meetha

500 grams dried apricots

¾ cup sugar

¼ cup fresh cream

1 Soak the apricots in three cups of water overnight or for at least six hours. Remove the seeds and crack them open to remove the kernels. Blanch the kernels, remove the skin and set aside for garnishing.

2 Boil the apricots for ten minutes in the same water in which they were soaked. Add the sugar and continue to boil till the sugar dissolves.

3 Remove from heat and cool slightly. Reserve a few apricots and purée the rest. Cook the purée and the reserved whole apricots over a low heat for five to seven minutes.

4 Serve, garnished with cream and apricot kernels.

chocolate nut fondue

1½ cups grated plain chocolate

8-10 almonds, chopped

5-6 cashew nuts, chopped

4-5 walnut kernels, chopped

1 cup fresh cream

Assorted fruit (such as plums, bananas, apples and peaches)

2 tablespoons rum or brandy

Marshmallows

1 Arrange the chopped nuts on an ovenproof baking sheet and roast in an oven at 180°C/350°F/Gas Mark 4 for ten minutes and set aside.

2 Place the grated chocolate in a double boiler. Keep stirring gently till the chocolate melts and the mixture is smooth. In a separate pan, heat the cream for one minute. Mix the cream into the chocolate.

3 Peel and cut the fruit into bite-size pieces.

4 Switch the fondue pot on, or place on a stand over a small burner. Pour the chocolate sauce in it. Add the rum and roasted nuts and mix well.

5 Pierce the fruit or marshmallows with a fondue fork and dip into the chocolate fondue. Eat at once.

mango bhapa doi with citrus fruit

½ cup mango pulp

1 cup thick milk yogurt, whisked

1 tin (400 grams) condensed milk

½ cup milk

A few peeled segments of orange

A few peeled segments of sweet lime

A few pomegranate kernels

A small sprig of fresh mint

1 Pour the condensed milk in a bowl. Add the yogurt, mango pulp and milk and mix well. Transfer the mixture into a steamer container.

2 Heat sufficient water in a steamer. Cover the container with aluminium foil and place in the steamer.

3 Cover the steamer and steam for twenty to twenty five minutes.

4 Cool and place in the refrigerator to set.

5 Unmould onto a serving plate. Arrange the orange and sweet lime segments in a decorative pattern all around. Top with a few pomegranate kernels. Place a small sprig of mint on top and serve chilled.

saeb aur sooji halwa

2 large apples, thinly sliced

+ 1 large apple, puréed

½ cup semolina

1 cup milk

½ cup sugar

½ teaspoon green cardamom powder

A generous pinch of saffron

5-6 pistachios, blanched and slivered

1 Dry-roast the semolina lightly, taking care that it does not change colour.

2 Boil the milk with one cup of water in a deep pan. Add the sugar, cardamom powder and half of the saffron.

3 Slowly add the semolina and cook, stirring, till it becomes semi-dry. Add the puréed apple. Cook for two to three minutes.

4 Divide into four portions. Pack each portion tightly into a bowl, turn it upside down onto a serving plate and unmould.

5 Decorate with apple slices, pistachios and saffron.

TAMARIND PULP

Soak 75 grams tamarind in 100 ml warm water for 10-15 minutes. Grind to a smooth paste and strain to remove any fibres. Store in an airtight container in the refrigerator.

DATE AND TAMARIND CHUTNEY

Wash, stone and chop 15-20 dates. Dry-roast 2 teaspoons cumin seeds and ¼ teaspoon fennel seeds. Cool and grind to a powder. Cook dates, 1 cup tamarind pulp, cumin and fennel powder, ½ cup jaggery, 2 teaspoons red chilli powder, 1 teaspoon dried ginger powder, black salt, salt and four cups of water till thick.

GREEN CHUTNEY

Grind together 1 cup fresh coriander, ½ cup fresh mint, 2-3 green chillies, black salt to taste, ¼ teaspoon sugar and 1 tablespoon lemon juice to a smooth paste using a little water if required.

RED CHILLI-GARLIC CHUTNEY

Soak 10 red chillies in 1½ cups of water for half an hour. Drain and grind with 12 large garlic cloves, and 2 teaspoons lemon juice to a fine paste. Add sea salt to taste and 1 teaspoon cumin powder and mix well.

MINT CHUTNEY

Grind 3 cups of chopped fresh mint, 2 cups of fresh coriander, 6 chopped green chillies, 1 medium onion chopped and 3 inch piece of ginger to a fine paste adding a little water if required. Add 2 tablespoons lemon juice, salt and 2 tablespoons of dried pomegranate seed powder. Mix well and serve.

KACHUMBER

Cut 1 medium tomato, 1 medium cucumber, 1 medium green capsicum, ½ medium white radish and 1 medium carrot, into ½-inch pieces. Mix the vegetables in a bowl and add 1 medium onion chopped, 2 chopped green chillies, 2 tablespoons chopped fresh coriander, 1 tablespoon lemon juice and salt to taste. Toss well. Transfer to a salad bowl and serve cold.

COCONUT MILK

Process 1 cup grated fresh coconut in a blender with ¼ cup warm water. Pass the ground coconut through a piece of muslin or strainer pressing firmly to extract all the juice, or first milk. Add a quarter cup of warm water to the strained coconut to get the second, thinner milk from the same solids.

VEGETABLE STOCK

Peel, wash and chop 1 onion, ½ medium carrot, 2-3 inch stalk celery and 2-3 garlic cloves. Place in a pan with 1 bay leaf, 5-6 peppercorns, 2-3 cloves and five cups of water and bring to a boil. Lower heat and simmer for fifteen minutes and strain. Cool and store in a refrigerator till further use.

CHICKEN STOCK

Boil 200 grams chicken bones in water for 5 minutes. Drain and discard water. Boil blanched bones with a roughly chopped carrot, celery stalk, leek, 2-3 parsley stalks, 6-7 black peppercorns, 5-6 cloves, 1 bay leaf and 10 cups of water. Remove any scum which rises to the surface and replace it with more cold water. Simmer for at least one hour. Remove from heat, strain, cool and store in a refrigerator till further use.

FISH STOCK

Place 200 grams fish bones, head, skin and any unutilised portions of fish in a pan with 5 cups of water, 1 medium onion, sliced, 1 large fresh button mushroom, sliced, 2-3 inches celery stalk, cut into ½-inch pieces, 1 bay leaf and 4-6 black peppercorns. Bring to a boil, remove any scum which rises to the surface and simmer for fifteen minutes. Remove from heat and strain. Discard the solids and use immediately.

Note: Fish stock should not be stored in the refrigerator as it smells and transmits its odour to other foods.

MAYONNAISE

Place 1 egg yolk, salt to taste, ¼ teaspoon each white pepper powder, French mustard and sugar and 1 teaspoon vinegar in a clean bowl and mix thoroughly with a whisk. Alternatively, process the mixture in a blender. Add 1 cup of oil, a little at a time, whisking or blending continuously, until all the oil is incorporated. Add 1 teaspoon lemon juice and adjust seasoning. Store in an airtight jar in a refrigerator.

CHILLI OIL

Cook 6 tablespoons of chopped dried red chillies in 1¼ cups of groundnut oil on low heat for at least ten minutes. When completely cold, stir in 2-3 tablespoons of red chilli powder and 1-2 tablespoons of sesame oil. Cover and leave to stand for at least twelve hours. Strain into a sterilised bottle and store in a cool, dark place.

POTLI MASALA

Mix 200 grams coriander seeds, 25 grams sandalwood powder, 35 grams dried vetiver roots, 35 grams bay leaves, 20 grams dried rose petals, 25 grams black cardamoms, 30 grams cassia buds, 15 grams cinnamon, 30 grams lichen/stoneflower, 35 grams kulanjan/pan ki jadi and 25 grams kapur kachri and store in an air-tight jar. When you need to use it tie a portion in a piece of muslin and put it in the water to be used for cooking.

NIHARI MASALA

Dry-roast till fragrant: 4 tablespoons cumin seeds, 4 tablespoons fennel seeds, 12-15 whole dried red chillies, 2 tablespoons cloves, 5 green cardamoms, 3 black cardamoms, 25-30 black peppercorns, 4-5 tablespoons poppy seeds, 2 bay leaves, 1 blade of mace, 2 tablespoons dried ginger powder, ½ tablespoon nutmeg powder and 4-5 cinnamon sticks. Add 4-5 tablespoons roasted split Bengal gram powder. Remove from heat and set aside to cool. Grind to a fine powder. Sieve the mixture and store in the refrigerator in an airtight jar.

WHITE SAUCE

Melt 1½ tablespoons of butter in a thick-bottomed pan. Add 1½ tablespoons refined flour; stir and cook the roux (butter-flour mixture) over low heat with a wooden spoon. When it develops a sandy texture, remove from heat and cool. Peel 1 onion. Wrap a bay leaf around it studding it with 2 cloves at the two ends. Bring 1½ cups milk to a boil with the onion. Remove the onion. Pour the boiling hot milk into the cold roux, stirring continuously, to prevent lumps from forming. Simmer gently for two minutes. Add a small pinch of nutmeg and season with salt to taste and ¼ teaspoon white pepper powder. Melt ½ tablespoon butter and gently pour over the top of the sauce to prevent a skin forming.

Variations:

1. Cream sauce: Add one-fourth cup of cream and two tablespoons of melted butter to the white sauce.

2. Parsley sauce: Add one tablespoon of chopped parsley to the cream sauce.

Red Chilli-Garlic Chutney

FISH SAUCE DIP

To make the fish sauce dip, grind together 2-3 fresh red chillies and 3 garlic cloves coarsely. Add ¼ cup sugar, 3 tablespoons lemon juice, 1 tablespoon vinegar, 3 tablespoons fish sauce and salt to taste and stir until the sugar dissolves

MASSAMAN CURRY PASTE

Cook 4 spring onions, finely chopped, 12 garlic cloves, chopped, 1 inch galangal, chopped, 1 lemon grass stalk, chopped, 2 cloves, 1 tablespoon coriander seeds and 1 teaspoon cumin seeds in a wok over low heat for about five minutes. Grind to a paste. Add 5 black peppercorns, 3 dried red chillies, soaked and chopped, and 1 teaspoon salt and grind again. Makes half a cup of curry paste.

RED CURRY PASTE

Pound, adding one by one, 10 dried long red chillies, seeded, soaked and drained, a large pinch of salt, 1½ tablespoons chopped galangal, 3 tablespoons chopped lemon grass, 2 teaspoons grated kaffir lime rind, 1 tablespoon chopped fresh coriander root, 1 tablespoon chopped red shallot, 2 tablespoons chopped garlic with a pestle and mortar, to a smooth paste. Alternatively grind all the ingredients together in a grinder till smooth. Makes half a cup of curry paste.

ENGLISH	HINDI
Allspice	Kababchini
Almonds	Badam
Apple	Saeb
Asafoetida	Hing
Baby potatoes	Chhote aloo
Bananas, unripe	Kachche kele
Basil, fresh	Tulsi
Bay leaf	Tej patta
Beans, cluster	Gwar
Beans, French	Farsi
Beans, sprouted	Ankurit moong
Bone marrow	Haddi ke andar ka guda
Breadcrumbs	Bread ka choora
Brinjal	Baingan
Butter	Makkhan
Buttermilk	Chhaach
Capsicum	Shimla mirch
Caraway seeds	Shahi jeera
Cardamoms, green	Chhoti elaichi
Carom seeds	Ajwain
Carrots	Gajar
Cauliflower	Phoolgobhi
Celery	Ajmud
Chicken	Murgh
Chicken breasts	Murgh ka seena
Chicken mince	Murgh keema
Chicken wings and shoulder	Murgh pankhari
Chicken, Boneless	Murgh boti
Chickpeas	Kabuli chana
Chillies, green	Hari mirch
Chillies, red dried	Sookhi lal mirch
Chillies, red fresh	Tazi lal mirch
Cinnamon	Dalchini
Cloves	Laung
Coconut, dried	Khopra
Coconut, fresh	Nariyal
Coconut, tender flesh	Malai
Coriander seeds	Dhania
Coriander, fresh	Hara dhania
Cottage cheese	Paneer
Crab	Kekda
Cream	Malai
Cucumber	Kakdi/kheera
Cudpah nuts	Chironji
Cumin seeds	Jeera
Curry leaves	Kadhi patta
Custard apple	Sharifa/Sitaphal
Dates	Khajur
Dill leaves	Suva bhaji
Egg	Anda
Egg white	Ande ki safedi
Egg yolk	Zardi
Fennel seeds	Saunf
Fenugreek seeds	Methi dana
Fenugreek, dried	Kasoori methi
Fenugreek, fresh	Methi
Fish, king	Surmai
Flour, gram	Besan
Flour, refined	Maida
Flour, wholewheat	Atta
Garlic	Lehsun
Gelatine	Sares
Ginger	Adrak
Gourd, bottle	Lauki
Gram, Bengal split	Chana dal
Gram, Bengal split roasted	Daalia
Gram, black skinless split	Dhuli urad dal
Gram, black split	Chilkewali urad dal
Gram, black whole	Sabut urad
Gram, green skinless split	Dhuli moong dal
Gram, green split	Chilkewali moong dal
Gram, green whole	Sabut moong
Grapes	Angoor
Honey	Shahad/Madh
Jaggery	Gur
Ladies' fingers	Bhindi
Lamb leg	Raan
Lemon	Nimbu
Lentils, split	Masoor dal
Lentils, whole	Sabut masoor
Lettuce	Salad ke Patte
Mace	Javitri
Mango, ripe	Aam
Mango, unripe green	Keri
Milk	Doodh
Mint, fresh	Pudina
Mushroom	Khumb/dhingri
Musk Melon	Kharbooj
Mustard seeds	Rai
Mutton, boneless	Gosht boti
Mutton, mince	Keema
Olives	Jaitun
Onion seeds	Kalonji
Onions	Pyaaz
Orange	Narangi/Santra
Papaya, unripe	Kachcha papita
Parsley	Ajmoda
Peas, fresh green	Taaze hare matar
Peppercorns, black	Kali mirch
Peppercorns, white	Safed mirch
Pigeon peas, split	Toovar/arhar dal
Pineapple	Ananas
Pistachio	Pista
Pomegranate	Anar
Pomegranate seeds, dried	Anardana
Pomfret	Halva
Poppy seeds	Khuskhus
Prawns	Jheenga
Prunes	Sookhe hue aloo bukhare
Pumpkin	Kaddu
Raisins	Kishmish
Rice	Chawal
Rice, parboiled	Ukda chawal
Rose	Gulab
Saffron	Kesar
Salt, black	Kala namak
Salt, rock	Sendha namak
Sandalwood	Chandan
Screw pine	Kewra
Semolina	Rawa/Sooji
Shallots	Chhote pyaaz
Soda bicarbonate	Meetha soda
Spinach	Palak
Spring onion greens	Hare pyaaz ki pattiyan
Squid	Samudra feni
Sugarcane	Ganna
Sweet lime	Moosambi
Tamarind	Imli
Tea leaves	Chai ki pattiyan
Tomatoes	Tamatar
Tomatoes, cherry	Chhote tamatar
Turmeric	Haldi
Vermicelli	Semiyan
Vetiver	Khus
Vinegar	Sirka
Walnut	Akhrot
Yogurt	Dahi